of
The Moon & Star

A Collectors Guide to Moon & Star Pattern Glass with Price Guide

by
George & Linda Breeze

4207 Fox Creek
Mt. Vernon, IL 62864

Photography By
Robert Albright
Mt. Vernon, IL

Printing By
Image Graphics, Inc.
Paducah, KY

Cover Design By
Bill Regenberg
Paducah, KY

All Rights Reserved
ISBN# 0-9649326-0-1

For additional copies call 1-618-244-9921 for a list of distributers in your area.

TABLE OF
CONTENTS

1. History of American Glass .... Page 3
   (reprint from L. E. Smith sales catalog)

2. The Magnificent Art of Handmade Glass .... Page 5
   (reprint from L. E. Smith sales catalog)

3. Origin of the "Moon and Star" .... Page 6

4. 1874 Catalog Page .... Page 11

5. Identifying Manufacturers .... Page 12

6. What is a flaw in Glassware .... Page 19
   (reprint from L. E. Smith sales catalog)

7. Price & Condition .... Page 20

8. Pricing to sell .... Page 23

9. How to Use Your Moon & Star .... Page 24
   (reprint from L. E. Smith sales flyer)

10. Origins of the Moon & Star .... Page 25
    (reprint from L.E. Smith sales flyer)

11. A Word About Lamps .... Page 26

12. National Moon & Star Collectors Club .... Page 29

13. Color Codes .... Page 30

14. Special Acknowledgement .... Page 32

15. Photo Section .... Page 34

16. Moon & Star Look a Like Items .... Page 95

17. Early Catalog Pages .... Page 97

18. List of Contributers .... Page 109

19. About the Authors and the Book .... Page 111

20. Description & Value Guide .... Page 113

21. Bibliography .... Page 127

The History of American Glass

Replica of America's first factory, a thatched roof "glasshouse" has been built in Jamestown, Va. and viewed by thousands of tourists. Industry was established by first settlers on this site in 1608.

Modern-day reproductions of Early American milk glass. A favorite at the turn of the 19th century, milk glass is popular for decorative use in today's homes.

For 350 years, Americans have been making glass, one of the truly indispensable materials of our time. This enterprise has had a long and colorful history, ranging from the crude production of glass beads for barter with the Indians to the brilliant flow of today's hand-made glassware. Undaunted by the hardships and hazards of pioneer America, early craftsmen laid the groundwork for mass production of quality glass. And over the centuries manufacturers perfected the art of turning a costly raw material into a useful object everyone can afford.

Glassmaking in America began in 1608 when Captain John Smith sailed from England to found a glass factory at Jamestown, Virginia. Captain Smith had been sent to Jamestown by the London Company, a group of businessmen who wanted to develop the raw resources of the New World. Glass production in England was handicapped by the lack of fuel for furnaces and a scarcity of sand, the stuff of which glass is made. America's virgin forests could provide an abundance of fuel and there was plenty of sand along the banks of the James River. Jamestown, itself, was situated on a peninsula which stretched into the river.

Captain Smith was no glassmaker. But he brought to the New World eight experienced Polish and Dutch glassmakers. He established these craftsmen in a clearing in the forest about a mile out of Jamestown at Glass House Point. A crude hut, about 37 by 50 feet, was erected. The hut had a thatched roof and open sides. It was the first glass factory in America, indeed it was the first factory in the New World.

Indian attacks and the terrible living conditions which plagued the early settlers eventually overcame this first glass factory. Other glasshouses sprang up but they could not survive the trying conditions of pioneer America. Some were wiped out by fire, others were abandoned when the forests around them had been used up for fuel.

In the next century, the 18th, American glassmaking was given fresh impetus by two German-born colonists. One was Casper Wistar, the other Baron Stiegel.

Wistar imported Belgium glassmakers to man his glasshouse in southern New Jersey. For 42 years he and his craftsmen turned out a steady stream of beautifully fashioned glassware. Baron Stiegel, perhaps the most romantic figure in the early history of American glass, established a glass factory near Lancaster, Pennsylvania. It was staffed by glassmakers from many countries. Like Wistar, he made beautiful bottles, window glass, goblets. The few examples of this work which remain are highly prized by museums and private collectors. Unfortunately, the American Revolution put an end to glassmaking for a time and factories went into oblivion.

In the early part of the 19th Century, American glassmaking began to hit its stride. Well-managed and prosperous glass factories were established around Boston, in Cambridge, Somerville and other suburbs. These efficient plants produced all kinds of glass — bottles, window glass, tumblers, stemware, tableware and lighting fixtures like whale oil founts and hurricane shades. The outstanding glass factory of its time was founded by Deming Jarves who started the Boston and Sandwich Glass Company on Cape Cod in 1826.

Crude but essential, glass pieces from period of early 1600's are the roots of today's American hand-made glassware.

Deming Jarves has been called the first "glass industrialist." He developed a method of pressing shape and design into glass by mechanical means, and thereby made the mass production of glassware possible. He was granted patents for his ingenious methods of turning raw glass into useful objects. By 1850 his glass factory was a model industrial plant visited by manufacturers from all over the world. The Sandwich plant was able to cut the cost of producing glassware to the point where "Main Street" could afford these useful and decorative objects. This native tradition of better glass continues in the glassware industry right down to the present day.

Twentieth-century American hand-made glassware is one of the foundations of good living. Out of a rare and costly substance, man has developed one of the inexpensive, indispensable materials of our time.

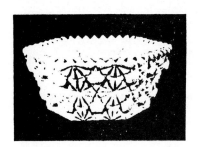

Today's glassware sparkles with beauty and is modestly priced. These hand-made glass pieces will blend in perfect harmony with any setting.

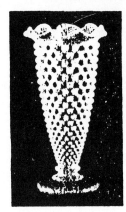

THE L.E. *Smith Glass* COMPANY
Westmoreland County
MOUNT PLEASANT, PA.

The Magnificent Art of Handmade Glass

Glassmaking is one of the most difficult, detailed and—finally—rewarding arts in the world. To begin with, the glass itself is not an easy medium in which to work. The <u>new</u> L. E. Smith Glass Company is indeed fortunate to be located in a region that offers the most important ingredient of glassmaking: experienced and dedicated craftsmen.

Many of our artisans are second and third generation glassmakers who have passed their wonderful handiwork and very specialized techniques down thru the decades. And although the <u>new</u> L. E. Smith can boast state-of-the-art technology that helps us produce consistent quality in the most efficient manner, the glassmaking techniques used by our craftsmen are virtually the same as those used in the 1880s.

History books confirm that much of the early American glassmaking took place right here in our home state of Pennsylvania, where the basic ingredients of glass—coal and sand—have always been plentiful.

The finest glassware has always been—and continues to be—made by hand. First the artisan takes his long, solid rod (called a "punty") and collects the right size portion (or "gob") from the "batch" of molten glass in the oven. Another craftsman (called the "presser") shears the gob from the punty and drops it into the mold, using an iron "former" or "plunger" to force the molten liquid into assuming the shape of the mold.

When the pressed piece of glass has cooled, it is passed to the "finisher" who works at the "glory hole," a small furnace in which he reheats the glass as he works with it. If this particular piece is to become, say, a basket, he must modify the shape and apply a handle. After the piece has gradually cooled in the "lehr," a tunnel-like oven with continuous conveyor belts, additional handwork such as etching or painting is performed. A special finishing technique called "fire polishing" can add to the permanent polish and luster.

The most remarkable thing about handmade glass is that, with so many teams of craftsmen and artisans involved in production, one piece so nearly duplicates the next. Often, what to the untrained eye may appear a flaw in the glass is instead the distinctive mark of the handcrafted process. This is why in all handmade products, slight variations exist in height or diameter or shape.

Your own eye and hand are enough to judge the real quality of handmade glass. Simply hold a piece of glass up to the light or against an all white background. Look for its clarity and luster. You'll see immediately why real handmade glass is such a prized possession in today's machine-made world.

Most of the early American glass companies have now disappeared, but L. E. Smith and its stable of superior craftsmen are proud to continue serving you with the very best handmade-in-America glassware available today.

ORIGIN OF THE "MOON & STAR" PATTERN

In the middle of the 1800's glassware production was drastically changed with the introduction of pressed glass!

Although most producers of the period used this method to copy or imitate cut glass, some insightful glass houses used this as an opportunity to produce a new and exciting type of glass, today known as pattern glass.

One of the first to use the new art form was Adams and Company of Pittsburgh, PA. John Adams was the head of the company. More can be learned about Mr. Adams and Adams and Company by writing the Carneige Library of Pittsburgh, PA.

Glassmakers of the period were quick to copy or imitate any pattern that was successful. In many cases this made it hard to identify the originating company.

One of the most successful patterns of this period was what we know today as Moon and Star.

First introduced by Adams and Company in 1874 in its catalogs and newspaper ads, its true name was "Palace."

The name Moon and Star was acquired very quickly from the design. Pressed into the glass was a round or circular depression with a star-like design in the center.

It did not take long for many other glass producers to try to cash in on the popularity and nickname. However, few ever became as popular as the original. We will talk about these a little more later.

Sixty-six original items were shown in the 1874 catalog. These included: a round butter dish, bowls, two cake stands, several sizes and designs of compotes, creamer, goblets, relish dishes, salt shakers, spoon holder, sugar bowl, juice, water and wine glasses, bread tray, salad bowl, syrup pitcher, and water pitcher.

As you can see, these items are tableware and were made to be used every day as were the reproductions. This has led to the loss of many of the original items through breakage throughout the years.

Although the quality of the glass and the method were well suited for color, all of the original pieces produced by Adams and Company were made of clear non-flint glass.

However, there are some indications that other patterns were produced in color before this time.

Some early Adams and Company pieces were decorated by undercoating, frosting and ruby staining. Records revealed that the ruby staining was done by the Oriental Glass Company and the Pioneer Glass Company, both of Pittsburgh, PA. Frosting was accomplished by applying acid to the parts to be frosted.

Although the glass was pressed in a mold, the glass was hand dipped, hand pressed, and hand crafted or finished after leaving the mold.

Handles from the 1800's were molded separately and applied while still hot to the glass and not molded as one piece as they are today. Most if not all of the Adams and Company handles were twisted before being applied. This will help to identify the Moon and Star items from the 1800's.

The production of one piece at a time and the hand crafting resulted in no two pieces being exactly the same. Not even in sets of goblets or plates.

Little is known about the production of the pattern from around 1900 until the 1930's. It is said that the size and weight made it costly to ship and therefore too expensive for most Americans of the time.

Our research shows that in the mid 1930's a young glass salesman named L. G. (Si) Wright had a brilliant idea.

Most of the glass plants of the day did not produce glass all year round. This meant that plants were closed and workers laid off until there were enough orders to start up the plant again. This meant that plants would lose good workers to other plants causing new unskilled workers to be hired and trained. This was very costly to the plants.

So, in about 1934 or 1935 Si Wright went to Mr. Frank Fenton, owner of Fenton Glass Company, with some molds that he had obtained from some glass companies that were going out of business. One of the molds was a Moon and Star egg cup mold that he had acquired from the Diamond Glass Company of Indiana, Pennsylvania.

The plan was for Mr. Fenton's company to produce items from Mr. Wright's molds during periods that the plant might otherwise have to close down due to lack of work.

The Fenton company would not have to shut down the furnaces or lay off workers that they might lose to other plants. This would save the company a lot of money in start-up cost. In return the Fenton Glass Company would produce the items for L. G. Wright at or near-cost.

From the Moon and Star egg cup mold, Fenton produced clear, unmarked egg cups, goblets, sauce dishes, and miniature night lamps.

When the items were produced, Mr. Wright stored them in his garage and would load up his old station wagon and set out across the country to sell them.

He would call on anyplace he thought might buy his glass -- places that had never thought about selling glass before, like hardware and lumber yards, florist shops, gift shops and department and clothing stores. Anyone that would listen, and possibly buy, he called on.

He mainly traveled the Southeast and Midwest in the early years.

This relationship was very important in the Moon and Star history from the 1930's to the 1960's. If not for L. G. Wright the pattern might have been lost altogether.

The location and ownership of all the original molds is not known. Some are rumored to have gone overseas and other are just not known.

In the 1940's the L. E. Smith Glass Company of Mount Pleasant, PA. engaged in the reproduction of early American pressed glass. While it's believed that these reproductions included Moon and Star, no records can be found to document it. However, catalogs from the early 1960's show the pattern in several colors.

It is also believed that some Moon and Star pieces from the L. E. Smith collection of the 1950's and early 1960's were made in Italy. A few collectors have items with "Made in Italy" tags on them. These are very rare and are very good quality glass.

The glass colors of the late 1950's gave new popularity to the pattern. This led many glass producers such as Smith to seek out new molds and ways to extend the pattern line.

In 1962 L. E. Smith Glass Company contacted Joseph Weishar of the Island Mould Company and contracted with them to produce some new Moon and Star molds. Island Mould Company would own the molds, and L. E. Smith would pay them royalties on every piece produced from their molds.

It was believed that the items produced after the 1930's were larger and heavier than the originals and led to the decline in the availability of the pattern during this time period. The weight caused the cost of shipping to drive the price up to the point that many of the original items were not feasible to produce. Although the weight remained the same in the 1950's, 1960's, and 1970's the methods and cost of shipping were now out weighed by the demand for the highly sought after pattern glass.

The Weishar family still owns and operates Island Mould Company and retains owner-ship to all the hand-chipped Moon and Star molds made by their father. In 1987 the family started producing miniature collector's sets of the Moon and Star water set. These had an outline of the State of West Virginia on the bottom with a "W" in it. In 1993 they started producing the collector's set of full-size water sets and compotes. These were made in limited sets and are marked with the Weishar signature on the bottom.

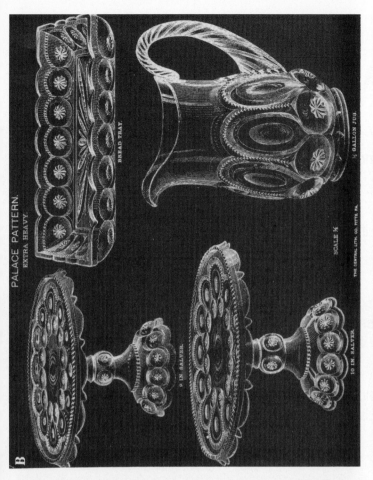

PALACE PATTERN.
EXTRA HEAVY.

SPOON.

SUGAR AND COVER.
Selt.

BUTTER AND COVER.

CREAM.

SCALE ¼.

THE CENTRAL LITH. CO. PITTS. PA.

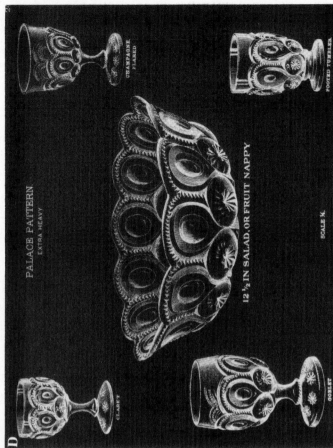

B

PALACE PATTERN.
EXTRA HEAVY.

BREAD TRAY.

½ GALLON JUG.

10 IN. SALVER.

9 IN. SALVER.

SCALE ¼.

THE CENTRAL LITH. CO. PITTS. PA.

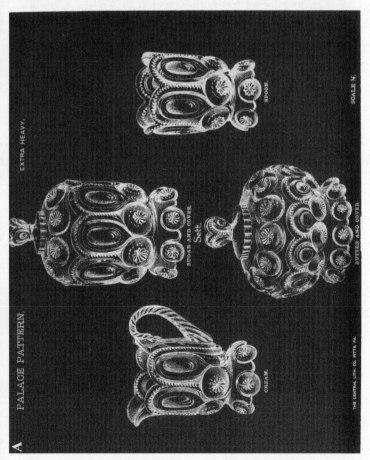

A

PALACE PATTERN
EXTRA HEAVY

VINEGAR OR OIL JUG.

SYRUP JUG SCREW TOP

LARGE EGG CUP.

CHERRY DISH

PICKLE DISH

9-IN. OBLONG PRESERVE

SHAKER TABLE SALT
OR PEPPER.

INDIVIDUAL
FLAT SALT

CELERY

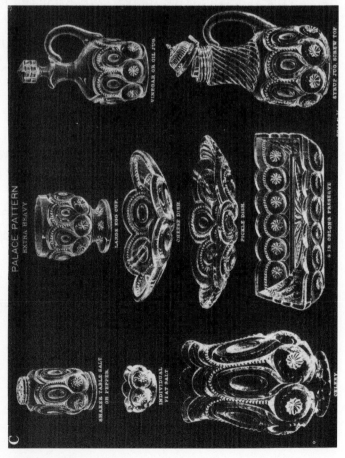

D

PALACE PATTERN
EXTRA HEAVY

CHAMPAGNE
FLARED

FOOTED TUMBLER

12 ½ IN. SALAD, OR FRUIT NAPPY

CLARET

GOBLET

SCALE ¼.

(Plates A-D) Assortment of Moon & Star pattern, reproduced today in color.

11

IDENTIFYING
MANUFACTURERS

Except for the Weishar Collectors series, almost all other items (with few exceptions) are unmarked.

Only a few of the many tens of thousands, if not hundreds of thousands, of pieces we have seen have not had a company mark.

One of these is the L. G. Wright mark. Many think that this is the Westmorland mark; they are close but not the same. The Westmorland mark is a circle with a "W" in the center of it. The Wright mark is a circle with a "W" in it with a line under the "W."

We have only found this on a few pieces and most commonly on the Vaseline. We have no date or time period other than the Vaseline was made in the 1968 -to -1970 time period.

The others that are marked are a few of the L. E. Smith pieces from the mid-1980's. These are marked with an "S" in the bottom. If you magnify the "S" you will see that in the top loop of the "S" there is a "G" and in the bottom loop of the "S" there is a "C;" all this for the Smith Glass Company . These were produced for only a short time period and makes them rare.

There is one other mark that we have seen and heard about that we're not sure of. A company named Levay Distributing in Edwardsville, Illinois had some Moon and Star items made in Amethyst Carnival by the L. E. Smith Glass Company. It is reported that some years they engraved the bottoms of their water pitchers to read something like "Levay 1976 1 of 150." This appears to have been done at Levay with an electric engraver. It is not very neat or easy to read.

It is almost impossible to identify many of the items by manufacturer unless you are educated on the colors and/or the items that the manufacturer made. We will get to this in greater detail later.

It is possible to identify some items just by color. Vaseline is a good example. L. G. Wright only made Vaseline; L. E. Smith did not. So, all Vaseline Moon and Star items are L. G. Wright.

Most Amberina items were made by L. E. Smith, and Most Ruby items were made by L. G. Wright. You will find L. E. Smith items that are Ruby, but they are not as common as the L. G. Wright Ruby items. And the opposite is true with the Amberina.

Milkglass or Milkwhite was made by both L. G. Wright and L. E. Smith, but all of the L. G. Wright items were made sometime before 1960 and L. E. Smith was made after 1960.

Many items that were made by both companies may look the same, but they call them by different names. For example, one will call their compote an 8-inch compote and the other will call it a 12-inch compote or candy box. They are both the same; one calls its size by the width and the other by its height.

Another good example are the goblets. One calls theirs a 9 ounce and the other an 11 ounce. I have taken a measuring cup and put the same amount of water in both. The 9 ounce will hold almost 11 ounces if filled to the rim, and if you pour 9 ounces in both they are filled to almost the same exact spot.

Your eyes would have to be a lot better than mine to see the difference in a lot of the items.

As you will see when you look at the photos of the L. E. Smith and L. G. Wright ashtrays, one calls theirs 8 inch and other 8 1/2 inch. If you turned one of them upside down on the other, you would find that they are the same size. If it were not for the difference in the patterns in the bottom of the ashtrays, you would not have been able to tell the difference.

I believe that this was done in a lot of cases to keep out of trouble with the owners of other molds.

In addition to Adams and Company, L. G. Wright, L. E. Smith and Fenton many others are rumored to have made Moon and Star in the 1950's, 60's, 70's and 80's.

These have included Fostoria, Kanawha, Westmorland, Libby, and Phoenix. It may be true that some of these companies may have made items for the L. G. Wright Company, but they are not known to have been producers of the pattern for themselves.

One big reason for this confusion factor is that L. G. Wright is not a glass producer or factory. They contract with other glass factories to make their products either from molds that they own or molds that the factory owns.

It is very possible that Westmorland could have made milkglass Moon and Star for L. G. Wright or L. E. Smith as they are known as a company who made a lot of milkglass.

Kanawha produced a pattern that looked like Moon and Star and still catches the uneducated buyer into thinking that they have found a rare or uncommon piece. The Kanawha look alike has the stars riding on top of the moons instead of being pressed into them. Their compotes have round knobs on the lids and bases rather square or flat sides like true Moon and Star. The colors are very close, and in some cases the same as Moon and Star. However, it does not have the value or popularity.

The Moon and Star of the 1800's likewise had companies that made look-a-likes or used names that came close. These included the: Wilson Glass Company, Co-Operative Flint Glass Company, National Glass Company, Boston and Sandwich Glass Company, and the New England Glass Company.

Such is the case of the National Glass Company. They made a pattern called Priscilla, called Crown Jewel in the 1896 catalogs, and later called Moon and Star by some and was tagged as "Late Moon and Star" in some sales materials.

We believe that a lot of confusion was caused with a pattern produced by the Wilson Glass Company named as Jeweled Moon and Star. The molds for this pattern were later sold to the Co-Operative Flint Glass Company and renamed as Imperial.

When the Co-Operative Glass and Flint Company went out of business, they sold the molds to the Phoenix Glass Company in about 1937.

The Boston and Sandwich Glass Company produced a pattern called Bulls Eye, and later the New England Glass Company produced Bulls Eye. It was also tagged as "Late Moon and Star." Some variations were called Bulls Eye and Star.

To date Bulls Eye is still the most confused for Moon and Star by dealers and collectors alike. The Bulls Eye punch bowl is sold hundreds of times a year as Moon and Star. Forty-nine out of fifty times a person who says that they have a Moon and Star punch bowl has a Bulls Eye.

The Bulls Eye is only about 8 or 10 inches across the center and smaller at the top in most cases because it is turned in. It has a row of circles around the middle on the outside. These are flat on top, and only every other circle has a star in it.

The true Moon and Star is much larger, around 12 inches across the middle, and when flared at the top, it could be 16 or 18 inches across. The Moons are closer to the base. The surfaces of the Moons are round, and every one has a Star in it.

Within the last year we have had all these patterns shown to us as Moon and Star when we asked dealer and collectors if they had any Moon and Star pattern glass.

Although there is a lot of confusion about who made what, there are only a few items that were made by both L. E. Smith and L. G. Wright that are similar. Most items can be identified by color or by the part number.

Of those items that are similar there are some tell tale signs that you can learn to help you.

ASHTRAYS:

If you will refer to the photos of the Smith 8-inch 6-sided ashtrays and the Wright 8 1/2-inch ashtray you will see that there are two that are very similar and one that has a different pattern in the bottom.

To better understand these you need to know a little something of the history of the L. E. Smith Company. About 1973 Smith was bought out by the Libby Glass Company. Libby owned Smith for 8 to 10 years. Before Libby bought Smith the 8-inch ashtray had a large star in the bottom like the Wright 8 1/2-inch ashtray does. Wrights has small stars between the points of the large star. Smith does not. That is how you tell the difference between the pre-1973 Smiths and Wrights.

In 1973 Libby changed the Smith ashtray bottoms to a small star in the center and surrounded it with tear drops. If you will look very carefully you will see that the area between the tear drops forms a star. This goes unnoticed by most collectors. So, items that have the tear drops in the center of the bottoms were made after 1973.

This applies to the 4-inch and 6-inch ashtrays as well as the Jardiniere.

GOBLETS:

If you will refer to the page that has the water goblets on it and look at the photo of the bottoms of the two goblets, you will notice that one is slightly larger than the other.

If you look at the group photo of the water goblets, you will notice that some of the goblets on the bottom row have thicker bases than the others do. See how many you notice.

The goblets with the thicker and larger bases are the L. G. Wright goblets. The others are the L. E. Smith ones. You should have been able to pick some just from the color. As we said earlier, L. G. Wright is the only one who sold Moon and Star in Vaseline. The dark blue is the L. E. Smith. This should make it easier for you next time you see one when you're out.

SALT DIPS:

Refer to the photos of the salt dips. The L. G. Wright tends to be slightly shorter and slightly bigger around.

Now refer to the photo of the bottoms of the salt dips. The L. G. Wright has a base about the size of a half dollar, and the L. E. Smith has a base about the size of a quarter.

SALT AND PEPPER SETS:

Refer to the photos of the salt and pepper. You should notice that one is just a hair shorter and bigger than the other . You should also take notice that the one has a flatter top and the lid sets in the middle of the shaker. This is the L. G. Wright.

The L. E. Smith tends to be straighter, taller, the top tapers in slightly, and the lid takes up almost all of the top.

You will also find that there are three styles of L. E. Smith lids. The oldest is believed to be about the size of a silver dollar and made of zinc with a chrome plating. It is the largest and heaviest of the lids. Next you will find them with the zinc lid about the size of a quarter. Last you will find them made of plastic and about the size of a quarter. The plastic lids may be stamped "Made in Hong Kong." This is the lids not the shaker.

This is believed to be the result in trying to keep cost down as time went on. The smaller lids were cheaper than the larger ones and the plastic cheaper than the zinc ones.

TOOTHPICK HOLDERS:

If you will refer to the photo of the toothpick holders you will notice that one has a flat bottom and the other has a scalloped bottom.

The scalloped bottom is the L. E. Smith and the flat bottom is the L. G. Wright.

If you find one that has a flat top and is just a hair taller than the others, it is not a toothpick holder. It is a cigarette holder or lighter holder from the earlier L. E. Smith smoke set. In later sets they used the toothpick holder with the scalloped top.

OTHER ITEMS:

Other items, such as compotes that were made by both are almost impossible to tell who made them other than by the color. If the colors were made by both, then it is very difficult and some we may never know.

It has been reported that on the L. E. Smith compote lids that the handles are taller than on the L. G. Wright ones. But I do not believe that this is a good way to tell most of the times.

It is also been said that L. G. Wright stemmed compotes do not have as clear a pattern on the stem. Again, I do not believe that this is a good way to tell.

I do believe that in most cases you will be able to tell because the item was not made by both companies or from color, size, and shape. You may find items that are not in this book. In those cases take a good look at the item. It may have been made from another piece by flaring the top or curving it in. There are a lot of items out there that were made this way.

What Is a Flaw in Glassware?

Is a small bubble in a fine piece of stemware a flaw? How about a cord, or a mold mark? The answer is definitely no, but it's sometimes difficult to convince a customer of this.

Most dinnerware and glassware departments and specialty shops have had trouble at one time or another with customers who seek flawless perfection in the tableware merchandise they buy.

Such perfection can be achieved only in assembly-line products, of course. It is not possible or even desirable in quality ware whose manufacture depends so much on the skill and artistry of individual craftsmen.

Slight variations and tiny imperfections in glassware pieces are actually a confirmation of craftsmanship and individual artistry. Most customers who appreciate good glassware understand this. For those who don't, here is a series of questions and answers that a salesperson can use to promote better understanding of the product.

Does a "seed" or bubble in glassware constitute a flaw?

No. One of these tiny "seeds" or bubbles the size of a pinpoint may sometimes be observed in a piece of glassware when it is examined closely against a strong light.

The bubble is formed by gases when chemicals are united in the fusing or melting of the raw ingredients. It does not affect the quality or the beauty of the glass.

Should all pieces in a set be exactly alike?

No. There are almost always slight variations in diameter, height, and other dimensions in any group of tumblers, goblets, plates, or other articles of glass. These variations are usually so slight that they can be detected only with a micrometer, rarely by the naked eye. This is the hallmark of fine hand craftsmanship.

What is a cord?

A cord is an almost invisible difference in density in the glass which occurs during the fusing of the molten glass. It is visible only by reason of the fact that it reflects light. When a goblet with a cord in it is filled with water, no light is reflected and the cord becomes invisible.

Is a mold mark a sign of imperfection?

No. A mold mark is merely a ridge on a molded glassware piece that indicates the point at which the mold that formed the item was separated for removal of the finished ware. If it is overly prominent, however, it may be an indication of careless workmanship.

What is a shear mark?

A shear mark is a slight puckering of the glass caused when the artisan snips off excess molten glass when shaping the piece, as for example the end of the handle of a pitcher. It is a normal characteristic of glass and should not be considered a flaw.

Is hand-made glassware really made by hand, or merely hand-finished?

The production of hand-made glassware is indeed a hand process. The skilled hands and eyes of many men, working in teams, go into the making of every piece. The amazing thing is that such a high degree of excellence can be attained; that piece after piece coming from any individual or group of glass blowers or pressers is so nearly and accurately a duplicate of every other piece.

Why can't small irregularities be entirely eliminated from hand-made glass?

For the very reason that the glass is hand-made. No matter how deft the touch of the sensitive hands of glass craftsmen, it is impossible to eliminate completely small variations. These should not, therefore, be considered flaws. Glass is one of the trickiest materials to work with. Even machine-made glassware cannot be made absolutely perfect. But consider this: even the finest diamond, examined under a jeweler's loupe, rarely reveals absolute perfection.

How can the salesperson and the customer judge the quality of glassware?

There are certain simple tests and guides. Look for clarity and luster by holding the piece against a pure white background. Good glassware is quite clear, while inferior grades show a cloudy bluish or greenish tinge.

Quality glassware is also marked by a permanent polish or luster that results from fire-polishing.

Look for smooth edges. Glassware edges should be even, never rough and scratchy. In hand-cut ware, the design should be sharp and accurate. In etched ware, each tiny detail should be distinct and clearly defined.

Fine handblown glass frequently contains lead, which improves its clarity and adds to its weight. If a piece of stemware rings with a clear musical tone when struck lightly, this indicates lead content. Lime glass, on the other hand, does not have this resonance, but this does not make it any less desirable. The lime in such glass adds to its toughness and strength.

Reprinted from
CHINA GLASS & TABLEWARES

PRICE
AND CONDITION

Prices contained in this edition are not guaranteed and will vary depending on area, condition, and color.

The prices are what we believe to be a good reference in the range that a buyer might find on the item in an Antique Mall or Shop and dealing with an educated seller.

We have collected prices from auctions, antique malls, antique shops, flea markets, other price guides when available, and from buyers and sellers who have related to us what they have paid and sold items for.

After gathering all the prices, we compiled a list and sorted through it. The very low and very high were removed from the list. The remaining sales were averaged to come up with the center price.

All sales above this figure were averaged together to come up with the high average price. All sales below the center average figure were averaged to find the low average sales price.

The low average sales price and the high average sales prices are what are shown as the most likely sales price range.

The popularity is growing on a daily basis. We have had to revise the price guide three times while waiting to get the book published, and the prices went up all three times. At the current rate of increase, it is expected that within a year, prices on some items may increase by as much as 50 percent.

In gathering the prices we found that there was very little difference in the value of most items by color. Amber, Amberina, Green, Blue, and Clear are the most common. Many items, such as some lamp styles, were only made in Amber and Green.

In some areas Green is the most sought after, in others, it was Amber. It seems to be based on decorating choices more than any other thing.

Some collectors only collect one color, others collect all colors. Some collect items for color only. I have never found a piece of Vaseline Moon and Star in a Moon and Star Collection. It has always been in Vaseline collections with other Vaseline patterns.

Some items may be higher than one would think because non-Moon and Star collectors collect them. Examples of this would be bells, salt and pepper shakers, salt dips and toothpick holders. So, not only are you competing with other Moon and Star collectors but other collectors also. You might not pay as much for a salt dip as a salt dip collector would pay if they needed it for their collection.

We attended a big glass auction in Southern Illinois. It had all kinds of cut and big name glass items. There were only three or four Moon and Star items. Two were blue salt dips. We stayed long enough for them to sell. There were four people there who collected salt dips we later learned. The pair brought $130.00! $65.00 a piece. At the time we thought that the price was unheard of, and we did not use these for setting the price. The buyer was happy. She did not have any Moon and Star salt dips and liked the pretty blue.

We also found that Amethyst, Ruby, Milkglass, and Vaseline always brought the highest prices in all parts of the country.

We collected price information from all parts of the country. The prices were higher in the Northeast, Southeast, on the Gulf Coast and the West Coast than they were in the Midwest. A price in St. Louis that might be outrageous, may be a bargain in Atlanta.

Moon and Star pattern glass was made to be used. Thus, it is rare to find pieces that are perfect in every way. As you read in the previous section some flaws or imperfections in glassware can make your collection special. No two pieces are ever exactly the same. I have a miniature amber oil lamp that has a bent stem and sets a little funny. I like it because it's different.

It is not uncommon to find a beautiful piece that may have some small chips or scratches. If we like it and the price, we buy it.

We use it in our home and office. We do a lot of holiday entertaining. Nothing helped set the Christmas tone more than Ruby, Green, Blue, Milkglass, Amber, Amethyst, Vaseline and Clear Moon and Star setting around with candy, mint, or nuts in them. Candle bowls and candlesticks with burning candles. Sugars and creamers setting on the table with nappys and bowls of chip and cracker with dips for the snacks. Makes you want to have a party so you can get all your Moon and Star out.

But almost all of these items that we use has a problem of some sort or another. A slight chip on the base or lid or something else that keeps it from being perfect.

We have our perfect items also, but we tend not to enjoy them as much because of the fear of breaking them. So they set on a shelf or in a box someplace.

Some may have air bubbles or mold marks (sometimes called straw marks). These things do not always take away from the value but makes your piece different from everyone else's.

Prices in this book are based on average condition. This means that they may have a minor flaw.

Some added value may be given for original boxes, labels, or items without defects.

You are the only one who can determine if a particular piece is right for you and your collection.

PRICING
TO SELL

One of the most common questions that we get asked is, "How do I price the items that I want to sell?"

The price guide will give you some help. But, we always tell people, that is a decision you have to make yourself. You know what you paid for the item. You know what will make you happy and how long you want to wait to sell it.

If you gave $1.00 for it and will be happy getting $2.00 for it, then that is what you need to price it at.

If the book gives $50.00 to $75.00 as the range, and you feel that you must have $100.00 for it, then that is what you need to price it at.

It may be that in your area the item may not sell for $50.00 to $75.00. It may be higher or lower.

But we all know that it will sell faster at $50.00 than at $75.00.

The sales price will also depend on how bad someone needs it for their collection. If we needed one more blue 13-ounce ice tea glass to finish a set, we would pay more for it than we would if we already had three sets of them.

Let your heart and your wallet be your guide.

How to Use
'Moon-and-Star'
to Enrich Your
Decorative Scheme

Only a few of the early versions (not Adams) of 'Moon-and-Star' were available in colors. This was unfortunate, since the smooth, round surfaces of the pattern are so well adapted to color.

To satisfy today's decorative demands, Smith Glass reproduces the pattern in six different colors. These are Amber, Avocado, Colonial Blue, Amberina and, in certain pieces, Crystal and Milk Glass. With this range it is possible to use 'Moon-and-Star' in almost any color scheme.

Because of the high cost and fragility of original 'Moon-and-Star' heirlooms they are used principally as occasional pieces or are safely ensconced behind cupboard doors. With authentic Smith Glass reproductions you can use this delightful pattern as it was intended by our forebearers. Certainly a large, colorful piece of 'Moon-and-Star' makes a beautiful decorative accent in almost any room. But a grouping, such as a compote and candleholders, or a table setting of tumblers or goblets, with other accessories, brings out the true harmony and utility of this handsome pattern. For luncheons and other informal affairs, a matching or contrasting table cloth and accessories often achieves a spectacular effect.

'Moon-and-Star' is perhaps the most versatile of pressed glass patterns for today's decoration. It is appropriate in traditional settings and it adds variety to contemporary styling.

By all means acquire some pieces of antique 'Moon-and-Star,' if you can, to go with your reproductions. Buy them from an established antique dealer, preferably in your own community. You and your friends will probably enjoy comparing the Adams product with Smith Glass. Both were handpressed, both were fire-polished to a fine lustre. The major difference, aside from cost, is that we have better control over the chemical ingredients—or "batch"—than did our 19th century counterpart.

Handsome 'Moon-and-Star,' in its choice of colors, provides pleasing decorative accents for a variety of settings.

24

The Enduring Pleasure of Handcrafted American Glassware

'Moon-and-Star' covered compote in amberina.

As our Nation grows older, young Americans are becoming more conscious of our heritage in the decorative arts. This is especially true of glassware. Collectors gladly invest their time and money in acquiring a representative group of a highly prized glassware pattern, such as 'Moon-and-Star.'

The increasing demand and rarity of "collectable" patterns has placed their cost beyond the means of most people who can enjoy them. This is unfortunate in two ways. First, it limits our appreciation of our cultural past; and second, it places an aura of reverence around early American glassware which does not belong there. Early handcrafted American glassware was made to be *enjoyed* and *used* . . . *not* revered. Pick up a 'Moon-and-Star' goblet or tumbler and you will realize that it was intended for the hand and lips of a youthful, robust, growing America.

For this reason, Smith Glass, in its *Heritage* reproductions, has set out to recapture the beauty and vitality of 'Moon-and-Star,' 'Daisy-and-Button' and other famous patterns. Our skilled craftsmen make this ware by hand, one piece at a time, using the identical methods employed for the originals generations ago. The cost of this handmade glassware is modest, thereby bringing the enduring pleasure of handcrafted American glassware within reach of all who love fine things.

Origins of
'Moon-and-Star'

Crystal 'Moon-and-Star' pieces reproduced from Adams' original designs.

'Moon-and-Star' is one of the patterns which came with pressed-glass method of producing glassware in the middle 1800's. Many of the later pressed patterns were imitations of cut glass. Not so with 'Moon-and-Star' . . . it was honestly and artistically designed to be pressed and, in many instances, further worked by hand to its final shape. Consequently 'Moon-and-Star' has a functional charm which appeals to our generation.

American glass houses of the 19th century did not hesitate to copy one-another's most popular patterns; and it is often difficult to determine who created a given pattern. The origin of 'Moon-and-Star' seems fairly well established. It was introduced by Adams & Co., of Pittsburgh, in 1874. The Adams trade catalog for that year listed the pattern under the name 'Palace' and showed 66 different pieces. About 20 years later the Pioneer Glass Co., Pittsburgh, and the Wilson Glass Co., Tarentum, Pa., brought out similar ware. Variations were made by other glass houses, but none had the beauty and lustre of the Adams' originals.

Through the years this pattern has acquired its popular name, 'Moon-and-Star,' by virtue of the principal design element pressed into its surface: a circular or oval depression with a star-like design — actually a rosette — placed in its center.

Anyone who is interested in learning more about early pressed glass will be rewarded by reading some of the excellent authors who have written on this subject. Among them are Ruth Webb Lee, Minnie Watson Kamm and, for milk glass, Eugene McCamly Belknap. Most of their books are in print or are available at the public library.

A WORD ABOUT LAMPS

One of the most prized Moon and Star items are the Lamps. Both oil and electric.

Both L. E. Smith and L. G. Wright made electric lamps of different sizes and shapes.

However, there is much confusion about lamps. You see Moon and Star lamp shades and fonts on all sorts and styles of lamps. We have seen Moon and Star pole lamps with one large shade or three smaller shades, pole lamps with Moon and Star fonts and glass shades and cloth shades, wagon wheel lamps with seven Moon and Star shades, Swag lamps and hanging lamps with and without Moon and Star fonts. Canister lamps with wooden bases and necks and cloth shades, Canister lamps with Moon and Star shades, 10-inch oil lamps with and without miniature shades.

In short, enough lamps to do a short book just on Moon and Star lamps.

But where did all these lamps come from? The Smith and Wright sales catalogs don't show all these lamps.

L. E. Smith and L. G. Wright are glass companies; they make money by selling glass. One of the country's largest buyers of glass is the lamp industry.

Both L. E. Smith and L. G. Wright sold glass lamp parts to lamp companies. Not just in Moon and Star, but in other patterns also. If you broke the shade on your lamp, you didn't go back to the store that you bought it at. In most cases you took it to a lamp shop for repairs or replacement parts.

In addition to lamp repair shops, they sold to large lamp manufacturers. They would design lamps and sell them to furniture stores and the likes. In many cases, the shade or font was the only part of the lamp that was Moon and Star.

Even when L. E. Smith and L. G. Wright made lamps, they were not always the same or had the same hardware, even if it is the same model number.

Glass is made in what is know as turns. A turn is four hours. They will only make things by turns. If you wanted to get a goblet made, they wouldn't set the molds up and just make one goblet. They would make them for four hours.

There is no way of knowing just how many goblets can be made in four hours. A lot of factors determine how fast they can be made on any given day. They can give it a pretty good guess, but it is still just a guess. They do not know how many will break or be so lopsided when they cool that they are unusable.

The same applies to glass lamp parts. Let's say, that the guess is that they can make 100 glass lamp parts in one turn of each of the parts needed to make a 24-inch L. G. Wright 90-series lamp. That would mean that they would need to make a turn of bases, fonts, and shades.

The guess was that 100 of each could be made in a turn, and they figure that they will have an unusable rate of 10 percent. That would leave 90 lamps that they could assemble and sell.

So, they order all the hardware to make 90 lamps. When they make the lamp parts they had a good day and turned out 130, with only five that they couldn't use to make lamps out of. They are now short on hardware for 35 lamps.

When they call the supplier, he does not have the exact same parts to make all the lamps the same, or he is out completely. They would go to another supplier and get the parts needed to finish the lamps.

Thus, lamps from the same batch could have different hardware parts. So, the same lamp made three years apart could very easily have different bases, or nipples, or shade holders.

Most lamps lose value after they are used, unless they are collectors' items like the Moon and Star lamps. Some times the value of the lamp is less than the value of the parts.

We have a 90-series ruby lamp without a shade. If and when we find one, the shade will most likely cost more than the original cost of the lamp.

I would not let the fact that a Moon and Star lamp had a different metal base or that the bulb socket was different than another that I had seen, stop me from buying the lamp if I wanted it.

Some lamps are seen with prisms. They did not all come with them. In most cases they were sold as an add-on kit that you could buy for a few dollars more when you bought your lamp.

Here again, you know if a lamp fits your needs or wants. Sometimes being a little different makes it worth more.

MOON AND STAR
COLLECTORS CLUB

While doing research and test marketing for this book, we met and talked to hundreds of Moon and Star collectors. One of the common questions we were asked was "Is there a Moon and Star Collectors Club?"

The answer was "No." So, in October of 1994, we formed the National Moon and Star Collectors Club.

The newsletter is produced quarterly and contains topics of interest to the members. Classified ads where members may advertise free Moon and Star items that they have for sale or want. Copies of old catalog pages and other information that members have requested.

If you would like more information on the Moon and Star Collectors Club or a free sample newsletter, write us at:

George and Linda Breeze
4207 Fox Creek
Mt. Vernon, Illinois 62864

or you can call and leave a message on the Moon and Star Hot Line (618) 244-9921 or call our home at (618) 244-3657.

CORRECTIONS, CHANGES, AND ADDITIONS

As with all things, we are not perfect. If you find an error or something that you feel has been left out that should be included in future updates, please contact us at the club number listed above.

We anticipate an updated version in three or four years, so help us get it right.

INFORMATION NEEDED!

We have had many requests for a book on Moon and Star from the 1800's to the 1940's. If you have any information, old catalogs, or glass pieces that you would allow us to use in our next book, please drop us a line or call us at the club number.

COLOR
CODES

There were many colors available during the 1950's, 60's, 70's, and 80's. Some were combined to give many wonderful combinations.

Next to the codes are listed the manufacturers that are known to have used these colors.

A=Amber - Smith/Wright/Weishar
AC=Amethyst carnival - Smith/Weishar
Am=Amethyst - Smith/Wright/Weishar
Amb=Amberina - Smith/Wright
Ambc=Amberina carnival - Smith
B Blue=(colonial blue) - Smith*
BO=Blue opalescent - Smith**
BLT=light Blue (Electric) - Smith/Wright
Br=Brown (aka Smoke) - Smith (1981 only)
BRO=Brown opalescent (aka Smoke) - Smith (1981 only)
BS=Blue Satin - Smith/Wright
C=Crystal - Smith/Wright
CC=Crystal Carnival - Weishar
CI=Cranberry Ice - Weishar
CO=Cobalt - Smith/Weishar
COC=Cobalt Carnival - Smith/Weishar
CL=Crystal Luster - Smith
CRO=Cranberry Rose Opalescent - Smith
CS=Crystal Satin - Wright
G=Green - Smith/Wright
GS=Green Satin - Wright
MGO=Mint Green Opalescent - Smith
MG=Milkglass (milkwhite) - Smith/Wright
MW=Milkwhite (milkglass) - Smith/Wright
P=Pink - Smith/Wright/Weishar
PC=Pink Carnival - Weishar

PH=Peach - Smith
PL=Peach Luster - Smith
PS=Pink Satin - Wright
R=Ruby - Smith/Wright/Weishar
RC=Ruby Carnival - Smith
RS=Ruby Satin - Wright
V=Vaseline - Wright
VO=Vaseline Opalescent - Wright
VS=Vaseline Satin - Wright

* L. G. Wright made a special order of water goblets for a restaurant that was very close in color to the Smith Blue. These are rare.

** Weishar made a Limited Edition Blue Opalescent. Weishar's is a dark blue, and Smith's Blue Opalescent is a light or electric blue

SPECIAL ACKNOWLEDGEMENT

Without the remarkable craftsmanship of moldmakers that expanded the Moon and Star line in the 1960's, this beautiful pattern glass would not be what it is today.

This, in the most part, can be credited to Joseph J. Weishar, owner of the Island Mould Company of Wheeling, West Virginia.

Mr. Weishar hand chipped and crafted most of the molds used by the L. E. Smith Glass Company. His artistic skill and vision to create the beautiful glass we so cherish today was truly a gift.

Mr. Weishar passed away in 1989, which was a great loss for the glass and mold industry.

Today, the Island Mould Company and the Moon and Star tradition is being carried on by his sons, Tom and John Weishar.

Without their assistance we would not have been able to provide you with all the valuable information that this book contains.

Tom and John are producing special Moon and Star Collectors series editions of some of the Moon and Star line, including miniatures. More information about these items may be obtained by writing:

Island Mould Company
84 Joan Street
Wheeling, West Virginia 26033

JOSEPH J. WEISHAR

Smith - 4286 4" 6-Sided Ashtray/Coaster

Smith - 4240 4 1/2" Oval Ashtray

Wright - 44-53 5" 6-Sided Ashtray

Smith - 4287 6" 6-Sided Ashtray

L - Smith - 4288 - 8" 6-Sided Ashtray - Post 1973; C - Smith - 4288 - 8" 6-Sided Ashtray - Pre 1973
R - Wright - 44-1 8 1/2" 6-Sided Ashtray

Smith - 4280 8" Round Ashtray

Smith - 5202 9" Banana Boat

Smith - 6212 12" Banana Boat

Wright - 44-32 11" Pedstal Banana Boat

Smith - 6222 4" Basket with Base

Smith - 6222 4" Basket without Base

Smith - 5207 9" Basket - Solid Color Handle

Smith - 5207 9" Basket - Clear Handle

Smith - 6219 11" Basket - Clear Handle

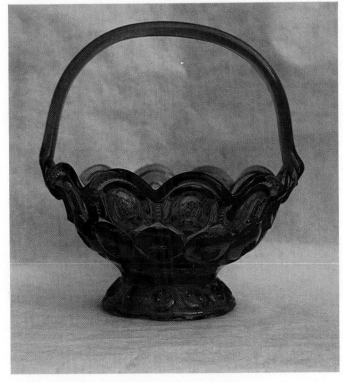

Smith - 5209 - 9" Basket - Solid Handle

Smith - 6125 - 6" Split Handle Basket

Smith - 6217 - 13" Banana Basket

Smith - 6235 6" Bell

Smith - 6229 8 1/2" 1/4 lb. Butter

Wright - 44-2 5 1/2" Round Butter

Smith - 4209 7" Round Butter

Smith - 4202 11" Low Cake Stand

Wright - 44-32 12" Low Cake Stand

Smith - 5232 11" Cake Stand

40

Smith - 6210 13" Collard Base Cake Plate

Smith - 6289 4-piece Canister Set

Smith - 5231 4 1/2" Candlesticks

Wright 44-4 6" Candlesticks; Smith - 5221 6" Candlesticks

Smith 5211 9 1/4" Candlesticks
Wright 44-3 9" Candlesticks

Smith - 5281 4 1/2 Candle Holder

Smith - 5217 5 1/2W 2" T Candle Holder

Smith - 6221 Candle Holder Nappy

Smith - 5205 7 1/2" Candle bowl; Wright 44-6 8" Candle bowl; Wright 44-5 9" Candle bowl

Wright 44-4-6 8" Console Set

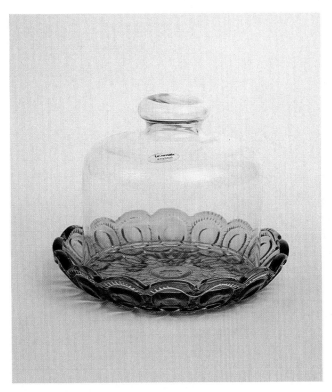

Smith - 4284 9 1/2" Cheese Dish

Smith - 4283 9 1/2" Footed Covered Cheese

Smith - 6224 6" Covered Compote

Smith - 5284 6 1/2" Covered Compote

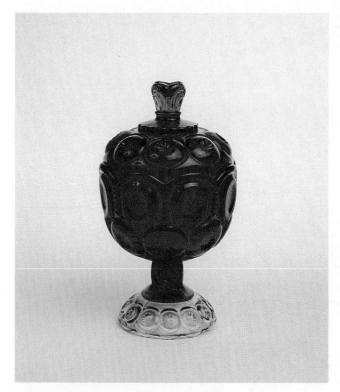

Smith - 5294 8" Covered Compote
Wright - 44-8 8" Covered Compote

Smith - 5204 7 1/2" Covered Compote
Wright - 44-10 7 1/2" Covered Compote

Smith - 4204 10" Covered Compote
Wright 44-9 6" W 10" Covered Compote

Smith - 6214 10" Covered Compote

Smith - 6204 12" Covered Compote; Wright 44-11 12" Covered Compote

Smith - 5283 4 1/2" Compote

Wright 44-12 8 1/2" Ruffled Compote

Smith- 5291 5" Crimped Compote

Smith - 5291 5" Scalloped Compote

Smith - 3601 6" 9-point Scalloped Compote

Smith - 3601 6" 18-point Crimped Compote

Smith - 4201 8" Flared Compote
Wright 44-14 8" Flared Compote

Smith - 4201 8" Rolled Edge Compote
Wright 44-14 8" Rolled Edge Compote

Smith -5201 7 1/2" Crimped Compote

Smith - 5201 7 1/2" Scalloped Edge Compote

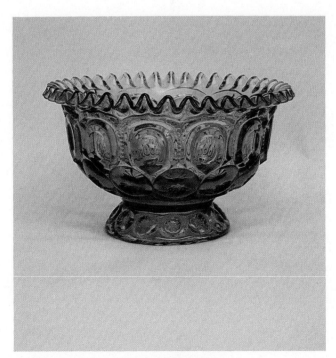

Smith - 6211 10" Crimped Compote

Smith - 6211 10" Scalloped Edge Compote

Smith - 6203 8" Scalloped Compote

Smith - 6201 10" Scalloped Compote

Smith - 4206 10" Rolled Edge Compote

Smith - 6206 12" Rolled Edge Compote

Wright 44-15 10" W 7" T Rolled Compote

Wright 44-14 8" W 5" T Open Compote

Smith - 42.61 3" Creamer and Sugar

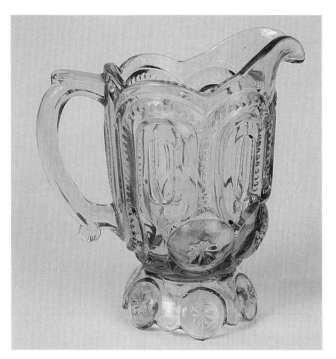

Wright 44-16 5 3/4" Creamer

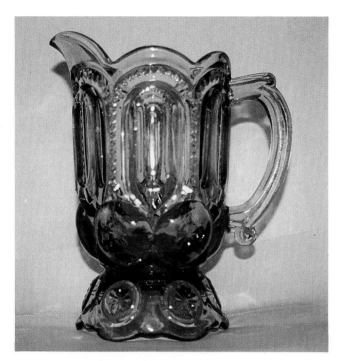

Smith - 4259 6 1/4" Creamer

Smith - 6241 6 3/4" Cruet

Wright 44-17 6 1/2" Cruet

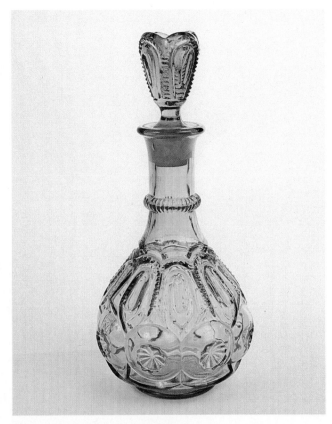

Wright 44-18 32 oz. Decanter

Smith - Decanter Set

Smith - 4282 9 oz. Dessert

Smith -4272 3 oz. Egg Cup

Smith - 5285 8" Tall Epergne

Wright 44-19 Epergne

Wright 44-21 Finger Bowl

Wright 44-45 Flower Bowl with Block

Wright 44-22 9 oz. Goblet; Smith - 3602 11 oz. Goblet

Smith Blue - Smaller Thinner Base; Wright - Ruby - Larger - Thicker Base

Smith - 4234 Large Jardiniere 9 3/4"; Smith - 4224 Medium Jardiniere 7 1/4" (Cracker Jar); Smith - 4214 Small Jardiniere 6" (Tobacco Jar)

Wright 44-24 Covered Jelly   Wright 44-50 8 1/2 T Footed Jelly

Smith - 6223 7 1/2" Oval Jewel Box

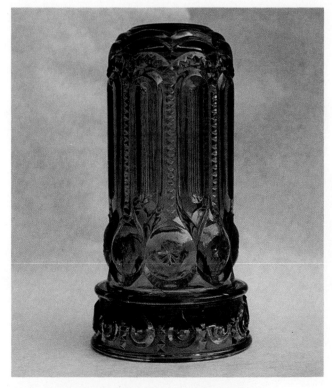

Smith - 6245 8" T Courting Candle Lamp

Smith - 6226 2 pc. 9" Candle Lamp

Smith - 5276 3 pc.
Matching 1/2 Shade
Candle Lamp

58

Smith - 6227 2 pc.
7 1/2" T Clear Base
Candle Lamp

Smith 6225 2 pc.
Courting Candle Lamp

Wright 44-FR 3 pc. Fairy Candle Lamp

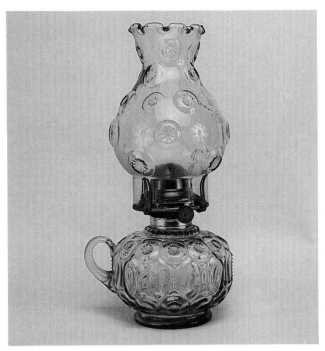

Smith - 4231 12" Oil Lamp with Fingerhold

Smith - 4231 12" Oil W/O Fingerhold

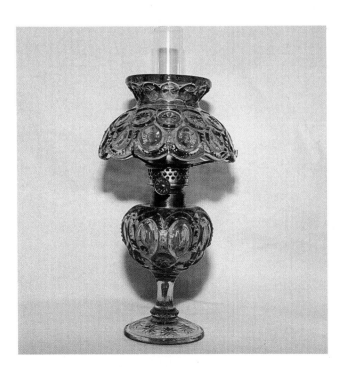

Wright 44-A 10" Mini Oil Lamp

Wright - 90 Series 24" Oil Lamp

62

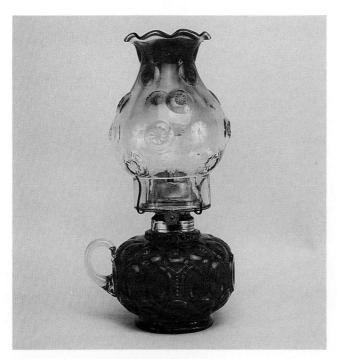

Smith - 4232 12" Electric Lamp

4249-24"

Smith - 4249 24" Electric Lamp
Smith - 4239 16" Electric Lamp

Wright - 90 Series 24" Electric Lamp

1000-MI
Height 30″
Moon & Star
14″ Dia. Shade

90-RG
Height 24″
10″ Dia. Shade

1000-MI-W/P
Height 30″
14″ Dia. Shade

90-G
Height 24″
10″ Dia. Shade

90-B
Height 24″
10″ Dia. Shade

90-A
Height 24″
10″ Dia. Shade

90-R
Height 24″
10″ Dia. Shade

Smith 4212 Lighter

Wright 44-43 6" W Nappy Crimpt

Smith - 6220 4 1/2" Nappy, Footed and Non-Footed

Smith - 5216 5 1/2" Round Handled Nappy

Smith - 6330 Powder Box

Wright 44-56 32 oz. Pitcher

Smith - 6228 40 oz. Pitcher

Smith - 6240 8" Dinner Plate; 1st Plate - Post 1978; 2nd Plate - Pre 1971; 3rd Plate - 1971-1978

Smith - 6240 7 3/4" Dessert Plate

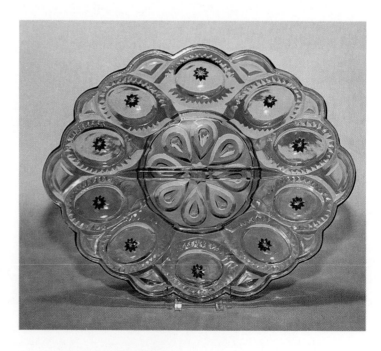

Smith 6250 13" Egg Plate

Smith Punch Bowl Set; 7101 - 14 pc. Cupped Set; 7102 - 15 pc. Cupped Set; 7111 - 14 pc. Flared Set; 7112 - 15 pc. Flared Set

Smith - 22" Punch Bowl Plate; Sold with 15 pc. Punch Sets

Left - Smith - Moon and Star Punch Cup; Right - Bulls Eye Punch Cup; Often confused for Moon and Star

Smith - Jardiniere Planters; 4238 - Lg.; 4227 - Med.; 4216 - Sm

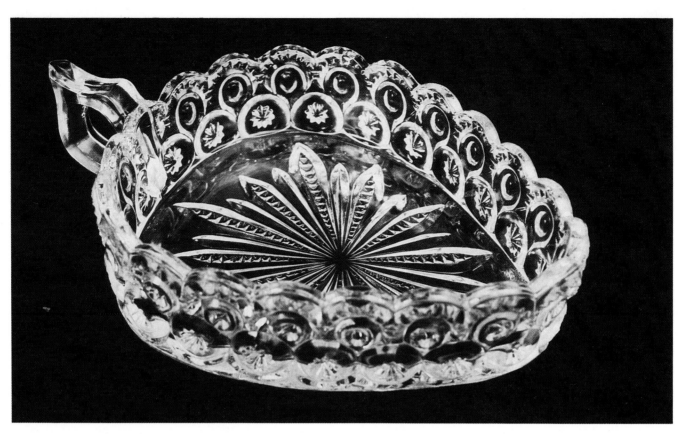

Wright 44-27 Triangular Handled Relish

Wright 44-40 Oval Boat Shaped Relish

70

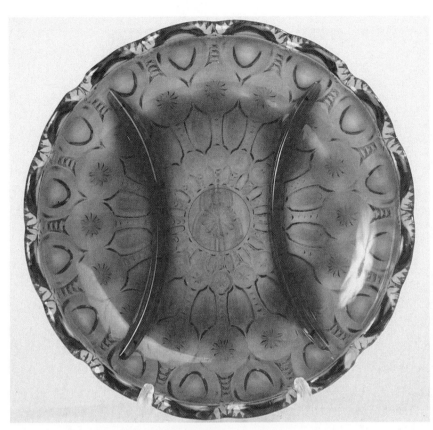

Smith - 4281 3 Part Round 8" Relish

Wright 44-28 8 1/2" Oval Relish

Wright 44-29 8" Rectangular Relish

Smith - 4200 4" Ring Holder

Smith - 4250 8" Jewel Tree

Wright - 44-44 Rose Bowl

Salt Dips; Smith - 5210; Wright 44-30

L - Smith - Small Base, R - Wright - Larger Base

Smith - 4251 4" Salt and Pepper

Wright - 44-31 4" Salt and Pepper

Smith - 4254 5" Salt and Pepper

Smith - 4425 5" Sugar Shaker
Smith - 4255 5" Cheese Shaker

Wright - 44-54 4 1/2" Sugar Shaker

Smith - 4256 5" Syrup Pitcher

Wright 44-35 Sauce Dish

Side View, Angle View; Wright 44-55 Flat Oval Soap Dish   Wright 44-36 Sherbert

Smith - 4292 6 oz. Sherbert   Smith - 4232 Stein/Tankard

Wright - 44-52 5 1/4" Low Covered Sugar

Smith - 5214 7" Covered Sugar

Wright 44-38 8" Covered Sugar

Wright 44-38 5" Open Sugar

Wright 44-37 Spoonholder

Smith - 4260 Spooner/Sugar

Smith Smoke Set; 4219 - 4 pc. Set; 4246 - 2 pc. Set

L - Wright 44-39 Toothpick Holder
R - Smith 4211 Toothpick Holder

Smith - 4222 11 oz. Tumbler

Smith - 4242 Old Fashion 11 oz. Tumbler

Smith - 4252 9 oz. Rocks Tumbler

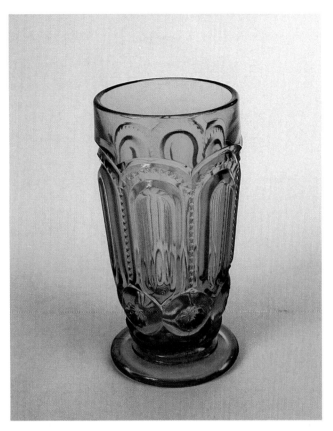

Smith - 6262 13 oz. Ice Tea

Wright 44-23 11 oz. Ice Tea

Smith - 6252 10 oz. Ice Tea

Smith - 6272 7 oz. Tumbler

80

Wright 44-41 7 oz. Footed Tumbler

Wright 44-25 5 oz. Tumbler

Smith - 6292 5 oz. Juice

Smith - 5271 Urn

Smith - 6231 6" Bud Vase - Flared

Smith - 6231 6" Bud Vase - Non-flared

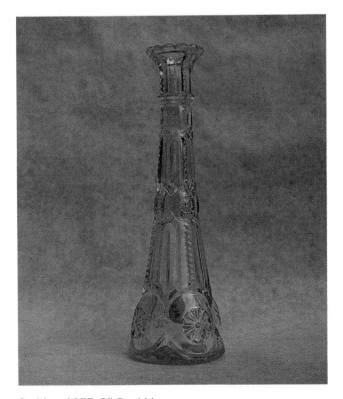

Smith - 6233 9" Bud Vase

Smith - 6263 7" Fluted Vase

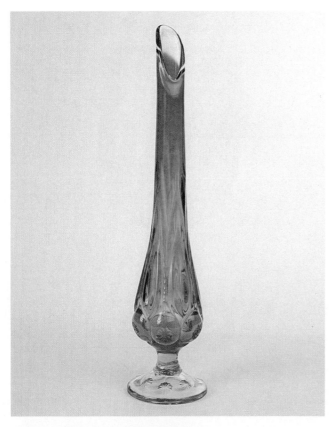

Smith - 5273 Goblet Base Vase

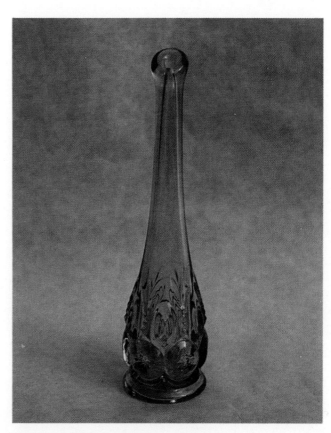

Smith - 5273 Toothpick Base Vase

Smith - 5261 8 3/4" Vase

Manufacturer Unknown; 7 1/2" T, 5" W, 7" L - Vase

Smith - 4272 3 oz. Cordial Wine

Smith - 4272 4 1/2" T Wine

Wright 44-42 2 oz Wine

Smith - 4262 6 oz. Claret Wine

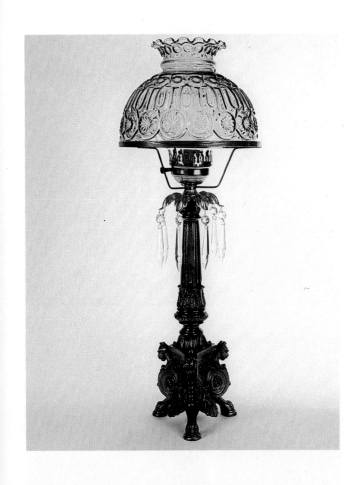

Various Moon and Star Lamps

85

Contributed Lamp Photos

First Canister Lamp Made By Joseph Weishar

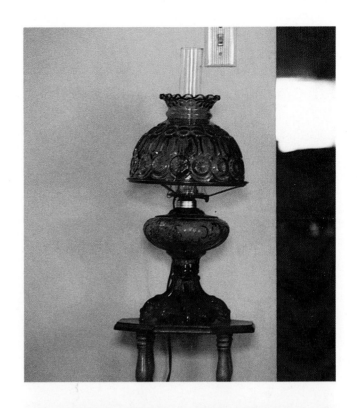

88

L. E. Smith Test Pieces

10" Plate Believed to be Wright

14" Plate Believed to be Wright

Wright 44-7 Champagne

Made from Wright Tall Jelly
Found in 6" & 8" Widths

Vaseline Moon and Star

Milk Glass Moon and Star

91

Tom and John Weishar - Owners of Island Mould, Inc., Wheeling, West Virginia

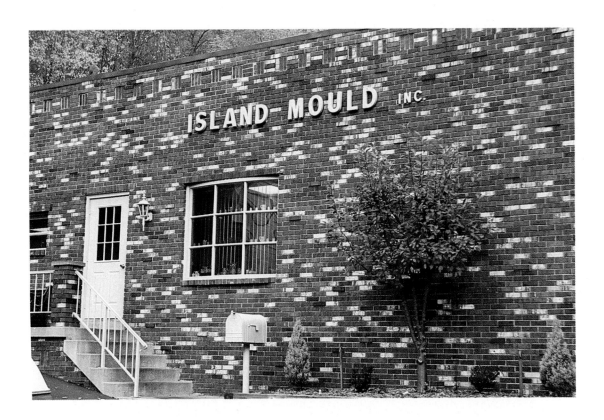

Weishar Collectors Series - Blue Opalescent; Only 200 Sets Made

Weishar Collectors Series - Cranberry Ice

L. E. Smith Glass Company, Mt. Pleasant, PA.

L. G. Wright Company, New Martinsville, West Virginia

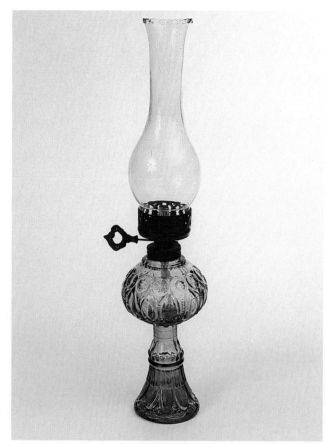

Moon and Star Look-A-Likes

Moon and Star Look-A-Likes

1967
MARKS
Smith's
60th Anniversary

Proudly we present the most complete line
in the history of handcrafted glassware.

Smith Glass NEW HERITAGE ITEMS FOR 1966

NO. 5283 — COMPOTE
Diameter 4⅝" — Height 4"

NO. 5285 — EPERGNE
Diameter 4⅝" — Height 8"

NO. 5281 — CANDLEHOLDER
Diameter 4⅝" — Height 4"

NO. 3282 — BASKET
Length 4" — Width 3¼" — Height 3¾"

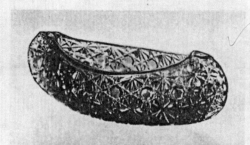

NO. 531 — CANOE
Length 6" — Width 2" — Height 2"

NO. 504 — HAT ASH TRAY
Diameter 3⅝" — Height 2"

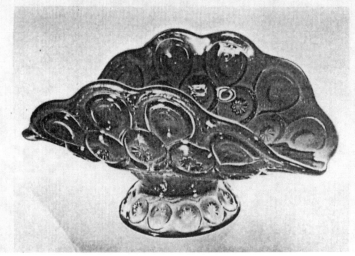

1968
Catalog Supplement

Moon and Star
Canister Set

Precision ground stoppers provide air-tight fit. Decorative as well as practical.

| 6285 | 6283 | 6282 | 6281 |
| 5 lb. | 3½ lb. | 2 lb. | 1 lb. |

——————— 6289 4 pc. Set ———————

THE L.E. *Smith Glass* COMPANY

MOUNT PLEASANT, PA. 15666

"Over a Half Century of Fine Handcrafted Glass"

NO. 7102 — 15 PC. PUNCH SET
12 Quart Cupped Bowl, 22" Flat Plate
12 - 6 Ounce Cups and Ladle
Packed Individually
Approx. Shipping Wt. 38 lbs.

NO. 7112 — 15 PC. PUNCH SET
12 Quart Flared Bowl, 22" Flat Plate
12 - 6 Ounce Cups and Ladle
Packed Individually
Approx. Shipping Wt. 38 lbs.

NO. 7101 — 14 PC. PUNCH SET
12 Quart Cupped Bowl
12 - 6 Ounce Cups and Ladle
Packed Individually
Approx. Shipping Wt. 22 lbs.

NO. 7111 — 14 PC. PUNCH SET
(Same as 7101 except with flared bowl)

COURTING LAMPS

A romantic new design in the Moon and Star pattern casts a diffused light throughout the room. These 8" tall Courting Lamps are gift boxed with 5" taper candles. The base is designed to also accommodate a pillar candle.

6245/9

6245/6

6245/1

6245/2

6245/5

6245/3

(Taper candle included)

BAG-O-LITE

Here's a clever little glass bag with a handcrafted edge to intensify the candle's glow. Packaged with a votive candle in its own burlap bag.

6576/2

6576/1

6576/9

3¼" high
(votive candle included)

SHOCK OF WHEAT

L. E. Smith used handcraftsmanship to harvest an autumn theme. Just 3½" high and complete with ball candle.

6552/5

6552/2

6552/1

3½" high
(Ball candles included as shown)

101

Country Brown

There's an exciting new color at Smith—COUNTRY BROWN. This neutral earth tone fits in with today's casual living. The kitchens and eating areas abound with shades of brown as this color trend establishes itself as one that will be around for some time.

MOON & STAR CANNISTER SET
6289/9—4 PC.

6285/9
5 lbs.

MILK CAN CANNISTER SET
7709/9—4 PC.
7708/9—3 PC.
(w/o 7701/9)

SPICES

6283/9
3½ lbs.

6282/9
2 lbs.

7705/9
5 lbs.

6281/9
1 lb.

7703/9
3½ lbs.

4292/9
MOON & STAR
SHERBERT

3602/9
MOON & STAR
GOBLET

4222/9
MOON & STAR
TUMBLER

7702/9
2 lbs.

6240 Moon & Star 8" luncheon plate also available.

7701/9
1 lb.

13

102

l.e.smith glass co.
MOUNT PLEASANT, PA. 15666 · 412-547-3544

Introducing 11 top-selling Moon and Star items in new PLUM color.

4201
8" Compote

5231
4½" Candleholder

5232
11" Skirted Cake Plate

5204
7½" Candy Box

5284
6½" Candy Box

6224
6" Candy Box

5291
5" Compote

5283
½" Compote

6222
4½" Basket

6220
4½" Nappy

4288
8" Ashtray

MOON AND STAR CRYSTAL

Whether it imbues old world charm on the dressing table or highlights an evening buffet, this fine selection of hand pressed gift items is a true classic in its own time. Your customers will appreciate that its meant to be used, collected, and enjoyed.

3602	11 oz. Goblet	5211	9¼" Moon and Star Candleholder
4200	4" Ringholder		
4201	8" Footed Compote	5214	7" Covered Candy
4222	11 oz. Tumbler	5231	4½" Candleholder
4281	8" Three-Part Relish	5284	6½" Covered Candy
4283	9½" Footed Covered Cheese	6220	4½" Nappy
		6223	7½" Covered Box
5201	8" Compote	6224	6" Covered Candy
5204	7½" Covered Candy	6235	6" Bell
5207	9" Basket	6250	13" Egg Plate
		6330	4⅛" Covered Box

6330

5207

Candle not included.

5211

Candle not included.

5231

5214

4200

6223

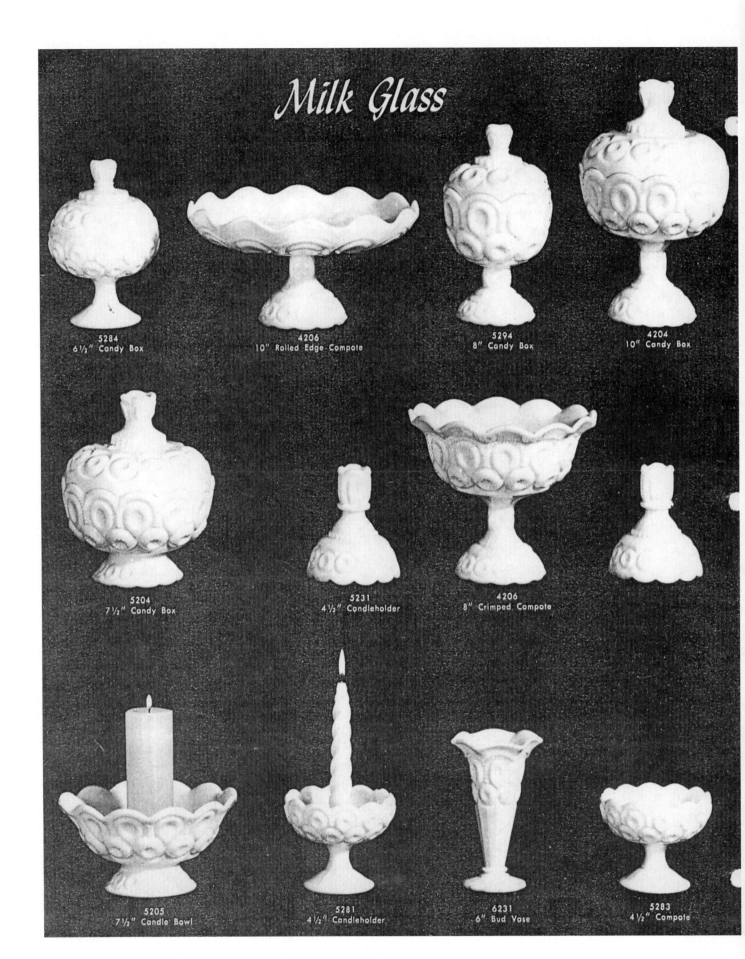

Milk Glass

5284
6½" Candy Box

4206
10" Rolled Edge Compote

5294
8" Candy Box

4204
10" Candy Box

5204
7½" Candy Box

5231
4½" Candleholder

4206
8" Crimped Compote

5205
7½" Candle Bowl

5281
4½" Candleholder

6231
6" Bud Vase

5283
4½" Compote

The
L. G. Wright
Glass Company

Cherished Today, Treasured Tomorrow

Moon
and
Star

44-22   Goblet

44-31	Salt & Pepper	44-23	Ice Tea
44-39	Toothpick	44-18	Decanter
44-35	Sauce	44-37	Spooner
44-54	Sugar Shaker	44-16	Large Creamer

44-52	Low Sugar w/Cover
44-50	4½″ Stemmed Jelly
44-15	10″ Open Compote
44-9	6″ Tall Compote w/Cover

44-2	Round Butter w/Cover	44-10	6″ Low Open Compote
44-42	Wine		
44-36	Sherbet	44-8	4″ Open Compote
44-38	Large Open Sugar	44-9A	6″ Tall Open Compote

THANK YOU

A special thanks to the following people who knowingly or unknowingly contributed to this book. Many people provided history, photos, and pricing information.

Dorris Allen	Water Valley, Tn.
Ann Andrews	Topeka, Ks.
Lynne Balsey	Shelby Twp, Mi.
Blanche Burns	Longmont, Co.
Betty Cain	Harrington, De.
John Cloud	Dekalb, Il.
Louis Corder	Mansfield, Mo.
Margaret Corso	Christopher, Il.
Kathy Crisp	Memphis, Tn.
Georgia Crowder	Mesa, Az.
Kathy Fleckenstein	Lacross, Wi.
Rex Hill	Coffen, Il.
Frances Horton	Sylacauga, Al.
The China House	Decatur, Il.
Don & Judy Hutchins	Ripley, Tn.
Jean & David Jaster	Levenworth, Ks.
Barbara Jeffries	Midland, Mi.
Bev Lambert	Selmer, Tn.
Regina Lambert	Stantonville, Tn.
Rochelle Larson	Albert Lea, Mn.
Lilia's Gifts & Coll.	Gallation, Mo.
Peggy McBee	Carterville, Il.
Larry McCormick	Dyersburg, Tn.
Gretchen Meyer	Milwaukee, Wi.
Geraldine Mier	St. Joseph, Mo.
Dayrl Nerness	Oscela, Ia.
Norma Richardson	Scheller, Il.
Elaine Roberts	Boyton Beach, Fl.
Janet Rutledge	Houston, TX.
Tracy Salava	Fairbury, Ne.
Sandy Sampson	Bosie, Id.
Harvey Snyder	New York, NY

Marilyn Stanton	Greenville, Il.
Ann Stark	Cross Timbers, Mo.
May Taylor	Memphis, Tn.
Patty Tyler	Adamsville, Tn.
Betty Viecelli	West Morland, Pa.
Billy Walker	Dyersburg, Tn.
Sandra Wallace	Selmer, Tn.
Barbara Woodward	Creal Springs, Il.
Caroline Yard	Taylorville, Il.
W. E. Wilman	Washington, VA

AND A SPECIAL THANKS TO:

The following gave many hours or their time trying to help us get it right. Many took us into their homes or businesses and allowed us to take photos of their collections. Some spent many hours taking photos and sending them to us or many hours on the phone at their own expense. We are deeply grateful for your help and support.

Dr. J. B. Scott	Odessa, Mo.
Corky Bunch	Warsaw, Mo.
Swinging Bridge Antiques	Warsaw, Mo.
BoJo's Antique Mall	Memphis, Tn.
Lorena Tunstill	Memphis, Tn.
Donna Wolford	Wichita, Ks.
Lois Bauer	Redding, Ca.
James Gibson, Jr.	Hammond, Il.
John & Doris Jenkins	Cayuga, In.
Andy Krietzer	Evansville, In.
Island Mold Co.	Wheeling, W. Va.
Red Roetteis	Albuquerque, NM.
Mr. & Mrs. Dale Wedge	Laughlin, Nv.
John Humpries	Chico, Ca.
Jim Anderson	Mt. Vernon, Il.

And a Thank you, Thank you, Thank you to: Dorothy Laur (Linda's mother), Donald & Edna Breeze (my folks), by brother Don Breeze, Nathan Breeze, our son, and our real estate company staff (Glenda, Mickey, Mona, Amanda, Pam, and Don) for putting up with our trips, taking Moon and Star calls for us and just helping out.

ABOUT THE AUTHORS
AND THE BOOK

Of all the parts of the book this is the hardest to do, and we have saved it till last (put it off is closer to the truth), and Linda is making me do it. Sounds like a wife of 25 years. She gets to do all the fun stuff, and I get to try and fill this page about us.

Linda and I both grew up in rural areas of Southern Illinois about 40 miles apart. We met as blind dates for a college spring dance. Linda was a nursing student, and I was a bum.

Almost 2 1/2 years later we were married. We have three children. Eric, our oldest, is a police officer in a small Southern Illinois town. Heather (our middle one) has finished college and is pursuing a career in broadcasting. This spring she presented us with our first grandchild (little William). So, Linda is a grandmother. (Told them they couldn't call me grandpa until I turn 50. We're only 44 and 46 now). Nathan, our youngest, is 17 and says he is leaving home as soon as he finishes school so that he won't have to take out the trash every week or fix me a soda when I get home from work.

After being married for three years, I joined the Navy. In 1989, after being stationed in several parts of the country, I retired in Virginia Beach, Virginia. Linda retired from nursing that same year and we ran a real estate company we had started a few years before we retired. In 1990 we were made an offer we couldn't refuse from an investment group to buy out our company. So, we sold out and retired again. This time we moved back home to Southern Illinois and now live only a few miles from our parents. We were too young to do nothing and within a few months, we started our own real estate company here and work together every day.

Linda has been collecting Moon and Star since she was a high school girl in the mid 1960's Me, I tried to collect other things at that age. The only moon and stars I cared about was the ones I tried, without a lot of success, to get some girl under.

After our return to Illinois, we started attending a few flea markets and started buying a few more pieces. One fall Saturday, we went to a flea market put on at one of the high schools about 30 miles from us. We saw a lot of Moon and Star and some strange stuff. It was a little higher than what we would normally pay for it, and because we hadn't seen any like it before, we decided it must be new. Now, we wish that we had bought it all. It was ruby and amethyst carnival.

The next weekend or so we went to Owensboro, Ky. Again, we saw some like we had never seen before, it was yellow. Again, we thought it was high, but I decided that I would by two pieces of it. That was all it took to turn me into a "Moonie."

We decided that before we went again, we should learn everything we could about Moon and Star. As most of you know, this was a tough thing to try and do. We bought every book we could find that had anything in it about Moon and Star. We wound up with a large pile of books and very little information. We called publishers, book dealers and even the factories. The results were the same. We had met several collectors during our quest for knowledge and when we related our story, they said they had lived it. I kept saying someone should do a book and everyone said the same thing, "You should do it."

So, we decided to do it. We have met and talked to hundreds and hundreds of collectors and all have contributed something.

A few common things kept coming up when we talked to them about doing a book. They would say "make the pictures larger and don't put 50 of them on a page" or "make the print larger and easier to read." We agreed, as our eyes are not as young as they were, and our arms keep getting shorter. Well, Linda's anyway, cause she is a grandmother.

So, that is what we tried to do. We met the publishers, and they didn't like the idea. It cost more to do a book that way. So, we decided to self publish. We hope you enjoy the book as much as we have meeting all those Moonies that have helped us put it together. God Bless.

ASHTRAY:

Smith 4240 $17.50 - $22.50
4 1/2" long oval shaped
A, B, BR, C, G 1968

Smith 4280 $25-35.00
8" d Round
A, B, BR, C, G 1968

Smith 4286 $15-25.00
4" d 6 sided, lg star in
bottom pre-1973, tear drops
in bottom post 1973
A, AMB, B, C, G, 1975

Wright 44-53 $50-75.00
5" d 6 sided, lg star in
bottom w/sm stars RARE
A, AMB, B, G, P, R 1968
C, 1977

Smith 4287 $50-75.00
6" d, 6 sided teardrop bottom Rare
A, B, BR, C, G 1982

Smith 4288 $35-55.00
8" d 6 sided, large star in bottom
pre 1973, Teardrop in bottom post
1973 Rare $50-75.00
A, AMB, AMH, B, BR, C, G 1967

Wright 44-1 $35-55.00
8 1/2" d 6 sided, Large star w/sm stars in bottom
A, AMB, B, G, P, RBY 1968
C, 1977

BANANA DISH:

Smith 5202 $25-45.00
9" long, collar base
A, B, BR, C, G 1968
AMB, 1975

Smith 6212 $65-90.00
12" long, collar base
A, B, BR, C, G 1975

Wright 44-32 $35-65.00
11" long on Pedestal

BASKET:

Smith 5207 $50-65.00
9" high solid handle
A, B, BR, C, G, R 1975
AMB 1979
Also made with clear handle on colored baskets,
rare $65-75.00

Smith 5209 $40-70.00
9" round basket matching or clear handle

Smith 6219 $65-95.00
11" round basket matching or clear handle

Smith 6125 $35-55.00
6" round basket split handle
or twig handle rare

Smith 6217 $65-100.00
13" Banana basket matching
or clear handle

Smith 6222 $25-35.00
4" Twig split handle
A, B, BR, C, G 1968
AMB , 1975

BELL:

Smith 6235 $45-60.00
6" tall
A, AMB, B, C, CS, G, P 1979
BO, BR, CO, MGO 1982

BUTTER DISH:

Smith 6229 $50-67.50
1/4 lb. oval 8 1/2" long
A, B, BR, C, G 1975
AMB 1979
Weishar BO 1991

Smith 4209 $50-67.50
7" round AKA covered cheese
A, AMB, B, BR, C, G 1968
AC ?

Wright 44-2 $50-75.00
5 1/2" d 6" h, round
A, B, C, P, PS, R 1968
PS 1971
VS 1971 $85-110.00
R 1969 $65-85.00
V 1969 $125-175.00

CAKE STAND:

Smith 5232 $75-95.00
11" d hi skirted rim, 2 pc.
A, B, BR, C, CO, G 1968
AMB 1979

Smith 4202 $65-90.00
11" d low, no rim
C 1968
A, AMB, B, BR, BRO, G, RBY 1982

Wright 44-32 $75-100
12" d low, 1 1/2" tall
A, AM, B, C, G, P, RBY, 1968
AMB 1969

Smith 6210 $70-90.00
13" high stimed

CANISTER, COVERED:

Smith 6281 $15-25.00
1 lb.
A, B, C, G, RBY 1968
AMB 1979
BR 1982

Smith 6282 $20-30.00
2 lb.
A, B, C, G, RBY 1968
AMB 1979
BR 1982

Smith 6283 $30-45.00
3 1/2 lb.
A, B, C, G, RBY 1968
AMB 1979
BR 1982

Smith 6285 $45-60.00
5 lb.
A, B, C, G, RBY 1968
AMB 1979
BR 1982

Smith 6289 $85-125.00
4 pc. Set
A, B, C, G, RBY 1968
AMB 1979
BR 1982

CANDLESTICK:
Smith 5231 $20-35.00
4 1/2" tall
MG 1963
BO, CO 1968
B, C 1975
MGO 1982

Smith 5221 $25-50.00
6" tall
MG 1963
A, B, BR, C, G 1968
AMB 1979

Wright 44-3 $50- 75.00
9" candlesticks
other than number, no other information found

Wright 44-4 $25-50.00
6" tall
A, AMB, B

Smith 5211 $50-75.00
9 1/4" tall
A, B, BR, C, G, P 1982

CANDLEHOLDER:
Smith 5281 $15-25.00
4 1/2" tall
MG 1963
AMB, B, G

Smith 5217 $35-50.00
5 1/2" W, 2" T fingerhold Nappy
A, AMB, B, C, G 1979

Smith 6221 $20-30.00
Nappy w/o fingerhold
A, AMB, B, C, G 1979

Smith 5205 $35-50.00
7 1/2" W candlebowl
MG 1963
A, AMB, B, G, 1979

Wright 44-6 $35-50.00
8" Console Bowl
AMB discontinued sometime before
1968

Wright 44-5 $50-75.00
9" Console Bowl
Discontinued some time before 1968

Wright 44-4-6 $120-150.00
8" console and 2 6" candlesticks
sold in set

CHEESE DISH:

Smith 4209
Covered, see Butter

Smith 4283 $75-$100
9" clear dome with pattern
base and candlestick base

Smith 4284 $65-85.00
Patterned base, clear dome 9 1/2" d
AMB, C, G 1982

COMPOTE:

Smith 6204 $100-150.00
12" tall 8" d
A, B, BR, G 1968
C 1975

Wright 44-11 $100-150.00
12" tall 8" d
A, B, C, G, P, RBY 1968

Smith 4204 $50-75.00
10" tall
MG 1963
A, B, BR, C, G, 1982

Wright 44-9/A $50-75.00
6" wide 10" t
A, AM, B, C, G, P, R 1968
V 1969 $125-175.00
VS 1971 $100-150.00

Smith 5294 $40-60.00
8" tall 4" wide
MG 1963
A, B, BR, C, G 1968

Wright 44-8/A $40-60.00
4" d 8" t
A, AM, B, C, G, P, R 1968
BS, GS, RS 1971
VS 1971 $85-120.00
V 1969 $100-150.00

Smith 5204 $45-75.00
7 1/2" tall
MG 1963
A, AMB, AMH, B, C, G, P, R 1968
BR 1982

Wright 44-10/A $45-75.00
6" wide 7 1/2" T
A, AM, B, C, G, R 1968

Smith 5284 $25-35.00
6 1/2" tall
A, AMB, B, G 1979
BR, C 1982

Smith 5283 $15-25.00
4 1/2" tall, open
C 1975
A, B, BR, G 1982

Smith 6214 $55-75.00
10" w 9" t covered
collard base

Smith 5201 $45-65.00
8" open scalloped or
crimped rim

Smith 6211 $55-75.00
10" open scalloped or
crimped rim

Wright 44-15 $65-85.00
10" d, 7" tall, open rolled
edge, scalloped rim
A, AM, B, C, G, P, R 1968
AMB 1969

Wright 44-12 $25-35.00
8 1/2" wide open ruffled rim
A, AM, B, C, G, R, P 1968

Wright 44-14 $55-75.00
8" wide flared rim 5 1/2" T
A, B, G, RBY 1968

Smith 3601 $20-30.00
6" tall, crimped rim
9 and 18 points
A, B, BR, C, G 1968

Smith 4201 $30-45.00
8" crimped rim
A, B, BR, C, G 1968
AMB 1979
MG 1963

Smith 4206 $65-85.00
10" rolled edge compote
A, B, BR, C, G 1968

Smith 6201 $65-85.00
10" crimpled edge
A, B, BR, C, G 1968

Smith 6206 $65-90.00
12" rolled edge compote
A, B, BR, C, G 1968

Smith 6203 $50-75.00
8" open, scalloped rim
B, C 1975

Smith 6224 $30-45.00
6" tall
A, B, BR, C, G 1968
BO, CO, MGO 1982

Smith 5291 $20-35.00
5" tall scalloped rim
flared bowl
AMB, B, C, CO, MGO 1975
BO 1982

CREAMER:

Smith 4261 $25-45.00
& Sugar Set 3" tall
A, B, BR, C, G 1968
MG 1963

Wright 44-16 $45.-75.00
3" d 5 3/4" t
A, B, C, P, R 1968
V 1969 $75-100.00
VS 1971 $60-90.00
PS 1971

Smith 4259 $45-75.00
6 1/4" tall 3" d
A, B, BR, C, G 1982
AMB 1979
AC ? *

CRUET:

Smith 6241 $45-75.00
6 3/4" tall
A, AMB, B, C, G 1975

Wright 44-17 $60-75.00
Round bulbous, pointed stopper
A, B, C, G

DECANTER:

Wright 44-18 $85-115.00
Bulbous, 32 oz. 12" T
A, AM, B, C, G, R 1968
(Ruby stoppers are clear, but should
match the M & S pattern)

Smith $65-85.00
Discontinued before 1965
made in Italy plastic cover
on stopper W/6 shot glasses.
A, B, G

DESSERT DISH:

Smith 4282 $35-50.00
9 oz.
A, B, C, G 1967

EGGCUP:

Smith 4272 $35-50.00
Footed 3 oz.
C 1975

Wright $50-75.00
none found
C

EPERGNE:

Smith 5285 $35-65.00
8" A, B, BR, C, G 1966
MG 1963

Wright 44-19 $75-125.00
AMH

FINGER BOWL:
Wright 44-21 $35-50.00
A, B, C, R

FLOWER BOWL W/BLOCK:
Wright 44-45 $55-75.00
with clear frog
R

GOBLET:
Smith 3602 $25-50.00
11 oz.
A, B, BR, C, G 1968
AMB 1975
AC
MG 1963

Wright 44-22 $25-50.00
9 oz.
A, AM, B, C, G, P, R 1968
V 1968 $55-85.00
BS, PS 1971
VO 1969 $65-100.00

JARDINIERE:
Smith 4234 $95-130.00
9 3/4" t 8 1/2" w
A, AMB, B, C, G, BR

Smith 4224 $55-85.00
7 1/4" T 6" W
A, AMB, B, C, G, BR

Smith 4214 $45-75.00
6" T 4 1/2" W
A, AMB, B, C, G, BR

Wright 44-24 $45-75.00
6 3/4" T 3 1/2" W
A, AMB, B, AM C, G, R

Wright 44-50 $50-80.00
8" T 4 1/2" W
A, B, G, P, R

JEWEL BOX:
Smith 6223 $80-125.00
7" long
C, P

LAMPS:
CANDLE:
Smith 5276 $55-75.00
3 pc. matching 1/2 shade
A, AMB, B, C, G 1975
BR 1982

Smith 6227 $35-65.00
2 pc., 7 1/2" tall, clear stim base
A, B, BO, BR, C 1975
CO, G, MGO 1975
MG base
AS, BS, GS, MWS

Smith 6225 $30-50.00
2 pc., courting
A, AMB, B, BO, BR, C, G, MGO 1975

Smith 6245 $45-75.00
8" tall courting
A, B, BR, C, G, R

Smith 6226 $45-75.00
2 pc., 9" tall M & S base matching
non M & S colored chimney
some had clear chimney
A, B, C, CS, G

Wright 44-FR $65-90.00
3 pc., Fairy lamp, 7" tall Beehive
ruffled round center piece
A, BS, R

ELECTRIC:

Smith 4232 $75-120.00
12" T matching Chimney
w & w/o thumb hold
same as 4231 oil only electric
A, B, BR, C, G 1968

Smith 4239 $150-250.00
16" tall M & S font
sold in amber and green only
A, G 1968

Smith 4249 $200-300.00
24" tall M & S font
sold in amber and green only
A, G

Wright 90-Series $275-575.00
Matching M & S glassbase 24" T &
10" M & S shade non M & S font
A, B, G, R

Wright 90-RG Series $325-575.00
Milkwhite non M & S base, rby non
M & S font and ruby M & S 10"
shade (also produced in AMH)

Wright 1000MI Series $275-375.00
30" tall 14" M & S shade
non M & S base and font
MG

OIL:

Wright 44-A $225-400.00
Miniature, footed, 10" tall
w/matching 1/2 shade
A, AM, B, MW, R 1968

Smith 4231 $70-135.00
12" tall, Bulbous base & matching
globe with & w/o thumbhold
A, B, BR, C, G 1968
AMB 1979

Wright 90-Series $250-400.00

LIGHTER:
Smith 4212 $35-60.00
A, B, BR, C, G 1968

NAPPY:
Smith 5216 $25-35.00
Round, pressed handle, 5 1/2" W
A, AMB, B, C, G 1979

Smith 6220 $15-30.00
w w/o base
A, AMB, B, C, G

Wright 44-43 $25-40.00
Crimped rim, 6" W
A, B, G, R 1968

POWDER BOX:
Smith 6330 $70-100.00
C, CO, P

PITCHER:
Smith 6228 $80-125.00
40 oz.
A, B, BR, C, G 1975
AMB 1979
AC * ?

Wright 44-56 $100-150.00
32 oz. 7 1/2" tall RARE
A, B, C, G, RBY 1968
P 1969

PLATE:
Smith 6240 $45-75.00
8" W, dinner, smooth rim
A, AMB, B, BR, C, G 1975

Smith 6250 $90-150.00
13" W, Egg
A, B, BR, C, G, RBY 1982
AMB 1979

Smith 6240* $60-90.00
7 1/2" dessert plate center
circle to hold sherbert dish
A, AMB, B, C, G

PUNCH BOWL SETS:
Smith 7101 $350-500.00
14 pc. set cupped bowl
no plate
C 1971

Smith 7111 $350-500.00
14 pc. set Flared bowl
no plate
C 1971

Smith 7102 $425-625.00
15 pc. set cupped bowl
22" plate
C 1971

Smith 7112 $425-625.00
15 pc. set flared bowl
22" plate
C 1971

RELISH:

Smith 4281 $25-45.00
3 part, round 8" W, flat bottom
A, B, BR, C, G 1968
AMB 1975

Wright 44-27 $50-75.00
Triangular 8" L, 2" deep
A, B, C, G, P

Wright 44-28 $30-50.00
Oval 8" L, 1 1/2" deep, 6" W
A, B, C, G, AM

Wright 44-29 $45-75.00
Rectangular, 8" L
A, AM, B, C, G

Wright 44-40 $75-135.00
Oval, Boat shaped
A, AM, B, G 1968
C 1974

RING HOLDERS:

Smith 4200 $30-45.00
Round 4" d
A, B, BR, C, CO, G, P 1982

Smith 4250 $100-150.00
8" Jewel Tree
A, AMB, B, C Very Rare

PLANTERS:

Smith 4238 $85-125.00
6 1/2" T, 8" W

Smith 4227 $55-85.00
4 1/2" T, 6" W

Smith 4216 $40-55.00
4 1/2" W

ROSE BOWL:

Wright 44-44 $40-55.00
A, G 1984

SALTS:

DIPS:

Smith 5210 $20-35.00
Small base; A, B, BR, C, G 1968

Wright 44-30 $20-35.00
Large base
A, AM, B, C, G, P, R 1968
V 1969 $35-50.00
VS 1971 $30-50.00

SHAKERS:

Smith 4251 $35-50.00
4" tall straight
A, B, BR, C, G 1968
AMB 1969
MG 1963

Wright 44-31 $35-50.00
4" tall
A, AM, B, C, G, RBY 1968
V 1969 $85-110.00
VS 1971 $80-100.00

Smith 4254 $50-75.00
5" Tall bulbous
A, B, BR, C, G 1982
AMB 1979

SAUCE DISH:

Wright 44-35 $25-40.00
Round base, scalloped 4 1/2" W
A, B, BR, C, G 1968

SHERBERT:

Smith 4292 $25-35.00
6 oz.
A, B, BR, C, G 1968
AMB 1979

Wright 44-36 $25-35.00
Footed, flared, 3 3/4" W, 4 1/4" T
A, AM, B, C, G, RBY 1968

SMOKE SET:

Smith 4246 $50-75.00
2 pc., lighter & 1 oval ashtray
MG 1963
A, AMB, B, BR, C, G 1967

Smith 4219 $75-95.00
4 pc., lighter, cigarette holder & 2 oval ashtrays
MG 1963
A, AMB, B, BR, C, G 1967

SOAP DISH:

Wright 44-55 $30-45.00
Flat, oval 6" L, 2" T
A, B, G, C, 1968
R 1969

SPOONHOLDER:

Smith 4260 $45-65.00
6" tall, footed
A, AMB, B, C, G 1979
AC * ?

Wright 44-37 $45-65.00
5 1/4" T, 3 3/4" D
A, B, C, P, R 1968
V 1969 $65-95.00
VS 1971 $55-85.00

SUGAR BOWL:

Smith 5214 $55-75.00
7" T, covered
A, AMB, B, C, G 1975
AC *?

Wright 44-38 $55-75.00
Covered 8" T, 4 1/2" D
A, B, C, RBY 1968
P 1969
V 1969 $75-100.00
VS 1971 $65-95.00
RS 1971

Wright 44-38 $35-55.00
Open 4 1/2" D
A, B, C, R 1968
P 1969
V 1969 $50-75.00
VS 1971 $45-70.00
RS 1971

Wright 44-52 $45-65.00
5 1/4" T, 4" D
Low covered
A, B, G, P, R 1968
C 1974
V 1969 $65-85.00
PS 1971

Wright 44-37 See Spooner

Smith 4260 See Spooner

SUGAR SHAKER:

Wright 44-54 $45-65.00
4 1/2" T, 3 1/2" W, bulbous
A, B, C, G, RBY 1968

Smith 4425 $45-65.00
5" T, bulbous
A, B, BR, C, G 1982

STEIN/TANKARD:

Smith 4232 $500-750.00
Only about a dozen were made and the mold
company has over half of them!
Very, Very, Very Rare

SHAKER, CHEESE:

Smith 4255 $45-75.00
5" tall bulbous
A, B, BR, C, G, R 1982

SYRUP PITCHER:

Smith 4256 $75-100.00
5" T
A, B, BR, C, G 1982
AMB 1979

TOOTHPICK HOLDER:

Smith 4211 $15-25.00
3 1/8" T, scalloped rim & base
A, B, BR, C, G 1968
AMB 1975
MG 1963

Wright 44-39 $15-25.00
3" T, scalloped rim, flat base
A, AM, B, C, G, P, R 1968
V 1969 $30-50.00

TUMBLER:

Smith 4222 $20-35.00
Water, 11 oz.
A, B, BR, C, G 1968
AMB 1979
MB 1963

Smith 4242 $45-60.00
Old Fashioned 11 oz.
A, B, BR, C, G 1982
AMB 1979

Smith 4252 $35-55.00
Rocks 9 oz.
A, AMB, B, C, G 1979

Smith 6262 $40-60.00
Ice Tea 13 oz.
A, B, BR, C, G 1975
AMB 1979

Wright 44-23 $35-55.00
Ice Tea 11 oz. 5 1/2" T
A, B, G, R 1968
C 1974
V 1969

Smith 6252 $30-50.00
Ice Tea 10 oz.
A, AMB, B, C, G 1975

Smith 6272 $30-50.00
7 oz.
B 1975

Wright 44-41 $30-50.00
7 oz. 4 1/4" T
A, B, G, R 1968
C 1969

Smith 6292 $25-45.00
Juice 5 oz.
A, AMB, B, C, G 1979

Wright 44-25 $25-45.00
5 oz. 3 1/2" T
A, B, G, R 1968

URN:

Smith 5271 $15-25.00
Footed
A, B, BR, C, G 1968

VASE:

Smith 6231 $25-35.00
6" T, Bud, scalloped rim
BO, CO, MGO 1982
C 1968
AMB 1979
MG 1963

Smith 6233 $25-40.00
9" Round, Pyramid shaped
A, AMB, B, C, G 1979

Smith 6263 $35-60.00
7" T, round base, fluted rim
A, AMB, B, BO, C, G 1975

Smith 5273 $55-100.00
9" Min., round base
A, AMB ?

Smith 5261 $75-100.00
8 3/4" tall, rare
A, G

WINE GLASSES:
Smith 4262 $27.50-45.00
6 oz. Claret Wine
A, B, BR, C, G 1975
AMB 1979

Smith 4272 $15-25.00
3 oz Cordial
A, B, BR, C, G 1968

Wright 44-42 $20-35.00
2 oz. looks like goblet
A, AM, B, C, G, P, R 1968
V 1968 $30-50.00
VO 1969 $35-60.00

Wright 44-7 Champagne $100-150.00
Discontinued before 1965

BIBLIOGRAPHY

Books

Bill Jenks & Jerry Luna. Early American Pattern Glass 1850-1910. Radnor, PA., Wallace-Homestead Book Co., 1990. A division of Chilton Book Co., pp 375-377

Bill Jenks, Jerry Luna and Darryl Reilly. Identifying Pattern Glass Reproductions. Radnor, PA., Wallace-Homestead Book Co., 1993. A division of Chilton Book Co., pp 224-233

Hammond, Dorothy. Confusing Collectibles. Des Moines, Iowa. Mid-American Book Co., Leon Iowa. Wallace-Homestead Co.,

Husfloen, Kyle editor. The Antique Trader. Antiques & Collectibles Price Guide Eight Edition. Dubuque, Iowa. Babka Publishing. 1991. pp 674, 675, 682

Kovels Antique and Collectibles Price List 1994. 26th Edition. New York, New York. Crown Trade Papers, Crown Publishing Co., 1993. pp 586-587

Fenton the First Twenty-five Years

William Heacock & Fred Bickenheuser. Encyclopedia of Victorian Colored Pattern Glass, Book 5, U. S. Glass From A to Z 1978. Antique Publications, P. O. Box 655, Marietta, Ohio 45750. pp 67

Glickman, Jay L. Yellow-Green Vaseline! A guide to the Magic Glass 1991. Antique Publications, P. O. Box 553, Marietta, Ohio 45750. pp 61 & 84.

GENERAL MERCHANDISE CATALOGS

Smith, L. E., Glass Company, Mount Pleasant, PA

1963-1964	Catalog and Price List
1966	Sales Catalog
1967	Smith 60th Anniversary Catalog
1967-1968	Sales Catalog
1968	Sales Catalog and Price List
1968	Sales Catalog Supplement
1970	Supplement
1971	Handmade Punch Bowl Sets Catalog
1971-1972	Sales Catalog
1972	Romance & Use of "Moon and Star" Hand Crafted Glassware.
1972	The Enduring Pleasure of Hand Crafted American Glassware.
1972	Origins of "Moon and Star"
1972	How to Use "Moon and Star" to Enrich Your Decorative Scheme
1973	Sales Catalog Supplement
1973-1974	Sales Catalog
1974	Sales Catalog Supplement and Price Guide
1977	Sales Catalog Supplement
1978	Sales Catalog
1978	Christmas Supplement Catalog
1979	Sales Catalog
1980	Sales Catalog
1980-1981	Lighting Shade Catalog
1981	Sales Catalog
1982	Sales Catalog
1984-1985	Sales Catalog
1986-1987	Sales Catalog

Wright, L. G. Glass Company, New Martinsville, PA.

1968	Master Catalog and Price Guide
1969	Catalog Supplement and Price Guide
1972	Catalog Supplement and Price Guide
1974	Catalog Supplement and Price Guide
1993	Master Catalog and Price Guide